Prophetic Words

For Daily Living

Dr. Rick Kurnow

Copyright © 2012

Dr. Rick Kurnow

All rights reserved.

ISBN-13: 978-1470076979

ISBN-10: 1470076977

Dedication

To my God and my Strength
My Deliverer and the portion of my heart forever.
Yeshua Ha Mashiach (Jesus The Messiah) The One who died for me and is alive today moving and filling my life through Ruach Ha Kodesh. (Holy Spirit)

"Whom have I in heaven but You? And there is none upon earth that I desire besides You. 26 My flesh and my heart fail; But God is the strength of my heart and my portion forever" Psalm 73:25,26

" But it is good for me to draw near to God; I have put my trust in the Lord GOD, That I may declare all Your works." Psalm 73:28

Prophetic Words

Table of Contents

All scripture quotations are from the New King James Version unless otherwise noted

Introduction – Speak to Me 1
The Joy of The Lord...2
I Will Make A Way For You...2
The Lord is My Rock..3
Don't Miss an Opportunity...4
Represent My True Character...5
Trust In Me..5
Listen to My Voice 6
I Am for you..7
Open Doors...7
Your Enemy Snared 8
Never Ending Love 9
Nothing Missing, Nothing Broken 9
Prosper 10
The Harvest Is Waiting...10
Shining Light in The Darkness 11
Do Not Be Afraid..11
Recover it All 12
Stand Still 12
A Prepared Bride 13
You Can Do It 13
I Will Deliver You..14
A Good Work In You...14
The Last Great Harvest..15
New Things I Declare..15
I Know you...16
A Place of Healing & Victory...16
My Strength in Your Weakness 17
More Than a Conqueror..17
Arise & Shine...18
I Am Your Treasure...19
I Will Build My Church 19
Prepare the Net...20
I Am With You...20
I Delight In You..21
I Have Specific Plans For You 21
I Do Not Change 22
Sing A Song To Me..22
The Plans of My Heart...23
Drink From The Fountain..23
Draw Near To Me...24
Dwell In My House..24
I Make All Things New...25
Trust In Me With All Your Heart..25
Today is a Good Day...26
Yes, Today is a Good Day...26
My Light is Shining in The Darkness 27

For Daily Living

Can You See Me Now?..27
Bring Your Offering..28
Let The Redeemed Say So...29
I Know My Plans For You..29
More Than a Conqueror..30
Trust in The Lord...30
I Work All Things Together 31
New Things I Declare...31
Fix Your Eyes on Me..32
Dwell in My House...32
My Grace is Sufficient..33
My Treasure in You..33
Better is One Day in My Courts...34
I Will Light Your Path..34
Nothing Is Impossible..35
I Work All Things For Your Good..35
I Will Shine Through You..36
Ambassadors..36
No Condemnation..37
My Divine Nature..37
Do Not Worry..38
I Have Come To Give Life...39
My Word Will Never Fail...40
All Things Are Possible With Me..40
Give Me Your Burdens..41
I Speak and it is Done..41
From Glory to Glory...42
Shine in the Darkness..43
I Have Betrothed You...44
I Will Supply...44
New Things I Declare...45
A Good Work In You...45
Times and Seasons are Changing..46
Your God Reigns..46
I Will Direct Your Steps..47
My Ways Above Your Ways...48
The Abundance of Your Heart...48
Do Not Fear Your Enemy..49
Draw Near To Me...49
Bear Much Fruit..50
The Victory Is Yours..50
I Am For You – Not Against You..51
Fix You Eyes On Me...51
I Have Chosen You..52
Dance With Me 52
Let Me Search Your Heart..53
I Speak and it is Done..53
The Word of My Power...54
You Are Not Alone...54
A Song In The Night..55
The Enemy Cannot Stop You..56
Be Healed...56
Do You Know I Love You?...57
You Can Trust Me..57

Rejoice	58
Sacrifices of Joy	58
Pure Unconditional Love	59
Sweet-Smelling Aroma	60
Behind The Veil	60
Bring Your Offering	61
Show Forth My Love	61
My Word	62
Shine Your Light	62
Delight Yourself in Me	63
Guard Your Heart	63
I Am The Lord Your Healer	64
The Path of Life	64
I Will Never Leave You	65
Do Not Be Afraid	65
Trust In The Name of The Lord	66
Now Is The Day of Salvation	66
Sacrifice of Praise	67
The Love of God In You	67
I Do Not Lie	68
Signs Will Follow	68
Make Known My Faithfulness	69
Trust Me With Your Whole Heart	69
Prophesy	70
Your Labor Is Not In Vain	70
The Crooked Places Made Straight	71
Goodness And Mercy	71
You Are More Than A Conqueror	72
Give And It Will Be Given To You	72
Hunger and Thirst For Me	73
The Desires of The Flesh	73
Care For Others	74
The Glories of Heaven	74
Many False Prophets	75
I Am Doing A New Thing	75
I Will Fight Your Battles	76
Soar Upon My Promises	76
The Rock of Our Salvation	77
Obedience Brings You Closer	77
Forget The Past	78
Dig Again The Wells	79
Walk According To The Spirit	80
Prepare For Famine	81
The Breath of My Spirit	82
The Treasure of Your Heart	82
The Just Live By Faith	83
Whoever Touches You	83
Rejoice!	84
I Am Love	84
I Will Fight For You	85
Yield and Be Obedient	85
A Land of Milk and Honey	86
Work While it is Day	86
I Will Bless You	87

I Will Not Withhold My Love..87
I Work Among a Perverse Generation...88
Bring Me a Sacrifice of Praise...88
I Am Your Deliverer..89
New Things I Declare...89
I Make All Things New..90
Cease From Your Dead Works...90
I Am The Way..91
I Reveal My Glory..91
Now is the Day of Salvation..92
My Word Abides Forever..92
Justified Through My Blood..93
I Will Fill You With Good Things...93
Rest and Quietly Trust...94
Don't Wait For Perfect Conditions..94
I Am Your Protector..95
Time Is Short...95
I Will Restore..96
You Are My Chosen...96
Abundance...97
I Do Not Condemn You...97
The Divine Nature...98
Rejoice In Me Always..98
About The Author..99
About The Author Continued..100

Introduction

Speak To Me

God wants to speak to you. He wants you to know how much He loves you. He also wants to give you direction for your life.

This book is a collection of "Prophetic Words" God has given me in my devotional times. As I read these words again, I was inspired, encouraged and uplifted. I experienced God's reaffirmation of His love for me and His desire to use me to make a difference in this world.

I want to share these words with you because they will do the same for you. My prayer is that God will use these words to help you draw closer to Him and to help you fulfill your calling and destiny in God.

These words are not to take the place of you reading your Bible. The Bible is the inspired Word of God and should always take precedence over any other writings. These prophetic words are based on scripture and I have carefully made sure that nothing written contradicts His Holy Word.

O LORD, You have searched me and known me. 2 You know my sitting down and my rising up; You understand my thought afar off. 3 You comprehend my path and my lying down, And are acquainted with all my ways. 4 For there is not a word on my tongue, But behold, O LORD, You know it altogether. 5 You have hedged me behind and before, And laid Your hand upon me. 6 Such knowledge is too wonderful for me; It is high, I cannot attain it. Psalm 139:1-6

The Joy of The Lord

"Do not sorrow, for the joy of the LORD is your strength."
Nehemiah 8:10

The Joy of the Lord is your strength. Live this day with joy. Let it spread to others as you praise Me. As you lift your heart in song. I AM the burden bearer. Therefore do not let the cares of this life steal your joy. You are my child and you are secure in Me. So rejoice! Sing praise! Shout aloud for you are victorious in Me. No battle will prevail against you, for I will fight for you and I have already secured the victory. Rejoice, rejoice, rejoice.

I Will Make A Way For You

He maketh my feet like hinds' feet, and setteth me upon my high places. Psalm 18:33 KJV

Put your trust in Me, and do not waver – for I will turn all things around for you. I will make a way for you where there seems to be no way. I AM opening doors of effectual service for you. You will discover a treasure of blessings that I have prepared and hidden for such a time as this. As you open this chest you will find a new joy. You will find a renewed vision as you venture on the adventure of your life. I will give you strength in this hour. Your hinds feet will propel you into the high places. I will use you to pour out my love on others and lives will be changed. Lives will be transformed. Rejoice for the river is flowing. The river is flowing. The river is flowing.

The Lord is My Rock

*"The LORD lives! Blessed be my Rock!
Let the God of my salvation be exalted." Psalm 18:46*

I AM the Rock of your salvation. My strength is made perfect in your weakness. I will revive and restore those things that have been stolen from you. I will make your feet like hinds feet in high places. You will catapult to a new level in me as I saturate you with my love. You will be filled with the fullness of who I AM. I will manifest Myself to you and through you. People will see My glory and blessing upon you. Rest in me. Do not try to make things happen. I will unfold all things perfectly and in my timing. Be assured you will not miss what I have for you. Jump into the river and go with the flow of My Spirit. I will take you places you never even dreamed you would go. Keep your heart in prayer and worship. Keep your heart pure before me. Do not be distracted in this hour, for I AM working a new work in you. You will present My heart and nature before others, and they will see me in you. I will touch the hurting and the maimed, the discouraged one through you. I will bring hope to the hopeless and you will see transformation before your eyes take place. All for My glory. All for My praise. All for My purposes.

Don't Miss an Opportunity

"Occupy till I come." Luke 19:13 KJV

Draw near to Me and I will draw near to you. I have been waiting for you. Remove the distractions for they cause scattering – but I AM a God of order and I have a season for all things. So much time is wasted. Time is a commodity I have given My people and so many waste it.. It is a commodity that you cannot get back once it is past – once it is used. So use your time wisely. For those who are diligent , they will reap a great harvest. Do not put off today what you can accomplish now. You may not have another opportunity. Opportunities sometimes come only once. Once it is past, it is gone and may not be retrieved. Look to Me and I will show you grace and mercy. I will redeem your time. I will restore the years that have been devoured. Behold I will do a new thing. I will give you a new beginning. I love you with an everlasting love, and my love transcends time and my love is not based on performance. But I do say lay up treasures in heaven where moth and rust cannot corrupt. Lay up treasures that are lasting and quit wasting time. For the time will come when I will call you home and time will be no more. Occupy until I come. Work now for the Day of the Lord is at hand. The earth is crying out in pain needing a redeemer. Who will go and who will tell them of my great love and plan of salvation. Go, I say and I will give you every tool and the ability to bring in a great harvest. I love you and I have chosen you for my glory.

Represent My True Character

"He who says he abides in Him ought himself also to walk just as He walked." 1 John 2:6

You are the apple of my eye. I chose you for My glory. I will instill in you a greater measure of My love. I delight in those who truly seek to represent My true character to the world. There are so many tainted and fragmented images of Me in this world. Many who call themselves my children do not truly represent the true nature and character of who I Am. I desire to show myself through you. Let Me shine brighter in your life. Let Me love through you. Ask the question daily and frequently. "What would Jesus do?" I will make you more like Me every day.

Trust In Me

"Trust in the LORD with all your heart, And lean not on your own understanding; 6 In all your ways acknowledge Him, And He shall direct your paths." Proverbs 3:5,6

Trust in Me and do not lean on your own understanding. I am forming and shaping your thinking, that you will think on things above and not on the things of the earth. Rely on Me and do not trust any other. Others will fail you and your expectations. But I will fulfill My Word in you, through you and for you. So trust in me. I Am a firm foundation and a shelter for the days ahead. Seasons change, people change. But I do not change. I Am the same yesterday, today and forever. My love is constant. My joy is sure. My strength is endless. I Am your everything. I Am your hope and your future.

Listen to My Voice

'My sheep hear My voice, and I know them, and they follow Me."
John 10:27

Walk with Me and listen to My voice. I will instruct you in the way that you should go. Trust Me for I know the plans I have for you. Plans to prosper and bless you. Plans to release you from all that tries to bind you. I will in this hour show forth my glory and all the earth will see it. Many walk in blindness but I will reveal myself in this generation. The wicked will not prevail but I will show my great love to a hurting and maimed people. I will instruct you in the way you should go and I will make your feet like hinds feet in high places. Look up for your redemption draws nigh. My Word will shine bright in the darkness and I will bring solution to every problem. Rejoice for in this hour I am releasing a great move of my Spirit and the church will arise in power. I am calling forth my bride and I will adorn her. I will give her beauty for ashes and the oil of joy for mourning and the garment of praise in exchange for the spirit of heaviness. I will comfort her in this hour of uncertainty in this world. For I will certainly take care of all that is mine and not one minute detail will be overlooked for I know all things and hold all things in my hands. I AM the Lord your God and I fail not.

I Am for you

"If God is for us, who can be against us?" Romans 8:31

There is nothing that I won't take care of in your life. I Am for you and not against you. I will unfold my plan to you. I will lead you by My Spirit into all truth. I will bless your going in and bless your going out. I will entrust you with My loving kindness. I will release you in my power. Rise up and rejoice in Me. Rise up and fulfill your call. Prepare yourself and be ready in season and out of season. Watch Me do more than you know how to ask me for.

Open Doors

"See, I have set before you an open door, and no one can shut it" Revelation 3:8

My ways are so far above your ways. I will bring you into a greater understanding of My plans for you. You will rejoice and be glad, for I will take you to many places. Many new places and many familiar places. I will equip you spiritually and financially. What door I have opened, no one can shut. I Am the Alpha & the Omega. The Beginning and the End. I will equip you in this hour. I will strengthen you in the inner man. You will rejoice and sing praises to me. I will give you a new song. A song of worship unto Me. A song of deliverance. A song in the night. You will rise up in My strength. Rejoice and be glad. I Am God and there is no other.

Your Enemy Snared

"Hear my voice, O God, in my meditation; Preserve my life from fear of the enemy. 2 Hide me from the secret plots of the wicked, From the rebellion of the workers of iniquity, 3 Who sharpen their tongue like a sword, And bend their bows to shoot their arrows -- bitter words" Psalm 64:1-3

*" But God shall shoot at them with an arrow; Suddenly they shall be wounded. 8 So **He will make them stumble over their own tongue**; All who see them shall flee away."* Psalm 64:7,8

Your enemy will be snared by his own words. They will backfire on him and the power of the decrees that he made against you will come back on him and bring you victory. Do not fear what the enemy of your soul will try to do to you. For I Am God and I Am your God. I have decreed good things over you and my declarations over your life will come to pass. I will shoot my arrows at your enemy and he will stumble over his own tongue. Put your trust in Me and know that I have numbered even the very hairs on your head. There is not a detail that can escape me. I know the heart and intent of the wicked, but I Am greater than any scheme or plot that would try to come against you. You are my child and I will protect and keep you in all of My ways. Come to me and rest in my arms of love. Know that my hand of grace and mercy rests upon your life and you are secure in Me.

Never Ending Love

"The LORD has appeared of old to me, saying: "Yes, I have loved you with an everlasting love; Therefore with loving kindness I have drawn you." Jeremiah 31:3

My love for you is a never ending fountain. It is moving it is fluid and it is not stagnant. I do not just say "I love you." But everything I say and do shows forth my great love for you. You are my child. I Am leading you by My Spirit. Be released into the fullness of all that I Am. Receive My love and let it spur you to action as you become a vessel poured out for My glory. Rejoice and be glad for you are my treasure. A diadem in My heart. I will form you, shape you and mold you after My image. My love for you is never ending.

Nothing Missing, Nothing Broken

"For as the heavens are higher than the earth, So are My ways higher than your ways, And My thoughts than your thoughts." Isaiah 55:9

My ways are far above your ways. I lead and I guide. I will lead and guide you into all truth. Rely on me and know that I love you with an everlasting love. My Word will be a lamp for your feet so that you will not stumble. Rest in Me and know that I Am your refuge and strength. I proclaim Shalom over your life, marriage, ministry and business. Nothing missing and nothing broken. I truly have used you to be a blessing in many people's lives, and I will continue to do so.

Prosper

"Beloved, I pray that you may prosper in all things and be in health, just as your soul prospers." 3 John 2

Live in My love. Walk in My love. Reach out in My love. I will fill you like a vessel that overflows and touches everyone and everything that comes your way. I will fill you with My love. A love that endures forever. Rejoice in Me and put your trust in me. You are chosen and called of me. I will make a way for you. I will open doors. I will lead you by My Spirit. Listen and obey. Listen and act upon the words that I speak that you may prosper and be in health even as your soul prospers. I Am Alpha and Omega. The work that I have begun in you, I will complete it. Rest in Me and in my love. Come away my beloved. Come sit at My feet and learn of My ways. Learn of Me. Draw near to Me.

The Harvest Is Waiting

"Do you not say, 'There are still four months and then comes the harvest'? Behold, I say to you, lift up your eyes and look at the fields, for they are already white for harvest"   John 4:35

The harvest is great but the laborers are few. Who will go for me? I say lift up your eyes and look and you will see that many are lost and need those who will lead them to Me. Will you go for Me? Will you trust Me for your every need? Do not waste time and do not wait for perfect conditions. If you do, you will not get anything done. Instead put your trust in Me and know that I Am God and I will work all things together for your good and My glory. I will supply all your need. I am just waiting for you.

Shining Light in The Darkness

" Unto the upright there arises light in the darkness.."
Psalm 112:4

My light shines in the darkness. My light will guide you on the path that I reveal to you. Keep your focus on me and do not be distracted. Look and observe and see that which I reveal on your pathway. I have prepared My purposes to come to pass. I will show you the way to go as I unfold my manifold wisdom regarding the issues of life that pertain to you and My kingdom purposes. So shine your light as I shine My light in you and through you and for you. Keep your eyes on Me and you will not stumble. You will not fall

Do Not Be Afraid

Fear not, for I am with you; Be not dismayed, for I am your God. I will strengthen you, Yes, I will help you, I will uphold you with My righteous right hand. Isaiah 41:10

I lift you up and redirect your pathways according to My will. Do not be afraid nor dismayed when opposition comes against you. But know I will give you wisdom and I will turn all things around for My glory. Put your trust in Me and rely on My wisdom. I make a way for you where there seems to be no way. My love is never ending and everlasting. I will fill you with My Spirit, wisdom and love. You will be a carrier of My glory, that others may look up and see that I reign in power and glory. I can turn the most impossible situations around.

Recover it All

"Pursue, for you shall surely overtake them and without fail recover all." 1 Samuel 30:8

You delight in Me, for I Am your strength and your song. I bring to light those things that need to be seen so that you can go forward in My purposes. I will always make a way for you. Trust Me and do not draw conclusions that come from carnal thinking. Instead, listen to Me. Listen and respond in faith knowing that I do all things well. I will never fail you nor my purposes. I will give you much favor in this hour. Reach out and follow Me. Do not wait for something to happen, but pursue and recover it all.

Stand Still

"Position yourselves, stand still and see the salvation of the LORD" 2 Chronicles 20:17

Put your trust in Me. Do not waver. Put your trust in Me. I am bringing you into a season of blessings. Receive My blessings and provisions, for they will propel you into My purposes. Stand still and see the salvation of your God. For I Am good and My love endures forever. I Am your treasure so delight in Me and no other. I will remove all that hinders you in this hour and you will rise in My strength. Nothing will be able to stop that which I have promised to do. Nothing!

A Prepared Bride

"Then I, John, saw the holy city, New Jerusalem, coming down out of heaven from God, prepared as a bride adorned for her husband." Revelation 21:2

This day have I created that many would be a praise to Me in the earth. I have much joy in My children and I am working in them. Crafted by My own hand. Created to reflect My glory. I am preparing My bride. I will present her before My Father. I have removed her iniquities and I have removed the residue of the stench of sin. No longer will sin have a reproach on her, for she is My bride. Pure and holy, filled with My character, My love and My virtues. Formed by My hand, protected and shielded from the schemes, tactics and devices of those who would seek to destroy her. I delight in My bride and I will cover her and protect her. I will fill her with wisdom. I will cause her to move in unity and love. I Am coming soon, and I will catch her up in My love. Eternity will be filled with the joy and celebration of My great relationship with My children who I redeemed to myself. Rejoice, for the day is coming soon. I Am waiting for the fullness of the harvest to come in. The precious fruit of the earth. I will not leave one soul out of heaven. I desire for the fullness of the harvest to come in.

You Can Do It

"I can do all things through Christ who strengthens me." Philippians 4:13

You can do it! Trust and Rely on Me! I will strengthen you.

I Will Deliver You

"Many are the afflictions of the righteous, But the LORD delivers him out of them all." Psalm 34:19

Many are the afflictions of the righteous, But I deliver them from all – out of them all. I Am working in you to bring about a great work. Please walk close to me and listen to me.. Take care of every area of your life. I will give you wisdom and knowledge. I will give you My love. Do not be afraid for I Am with you.. Do not stumble, but guard your heart and your thoughts. Keep My Word, follow My principles and you will not stumble but you will stand. Stand firm upon the foundation of My Word. Stand firm upon My promises. I Am the Lord your God and I fail not. I Am with you. Walk with Me. Listen to Me. Obey Me, and you will enjoy many blessings catered specifically for you. Those special things that minister to your heart. Walk in My supernatural power every day. Supernatural is natural. Love Jesus!

A Good Work In You

"Being confident of this very thing, that He who has begun a good work in you will complete it until the day of Jesus Christ;" Philippians 1:6

My heart towards you and all My children will always be faithful and true. I Am working in you, and I will complete the good work I began in you. Look to Me for all things. For in all things I will work together for your good and My glory. Look to Me and be filled with good things.

The Last Great Harvest

"But when the grain ripens, immediately he puts in the sickle, because the harvest has come." Mark 4:29

Live for Me and walk with Me. For this is a great hour. This is a pivotal time for the last great harvest of the earth. I Am strategically changing lives and nations. Those things that seemed impossible, I will make possible. Those things that seemed like they would never change, will change. I will transform cities and nations. No longer will things appear unclear and gray. I will make them clear and black and white. My people will arise in this hour and do exploits. Arise My sons and daughters. Arise and let My light shine brightly in you. Through you My light will expel the darkness and My kingdom will be established in this earth as it is in heaven.

New Things I Declare

"Behold, the former things have come to pass, And new things I declare; Before they spring forth I tell you of them." Isaiah 42:9

Rejoice and be glad for the former things have come to pass and new things I declare to you. Prepare your heart and get ready for changes. My changes always bring about the greater good and advances My kingdom purposes. Rejoice and be glad for I Am renewing your vision. Rejoice for the former things have been completed and I Am doing a new thing. Things that will bless you and advance My kingdom. I will unfold every day My plan. Be obedient and I will prosper you for My glory.

I Know you

"Before I formed you in the womb I knew you; Before you were born I sanctified you; I ordained you a prophet to the nations."Jeremiah 1:5

Before the worlds were made, I knew you. I ordained that you would come forth – for such a time as this. I have established you and I will bless you. I will give you My anointing and My presence. You will rejoice before me with songs of praise and adoration. I have given you My presence and My Spirit. So rejoice- for your God has given you favor. You will walk with Me in high places. You will declare all that I Am. Many will take hold of Me and My ways and my truths will establish every wandering soul. I will fill and multiply My people. Who will oppose Me? Who can withstand Me? Who can frustrate My divine plan and intervention. I Am Jehovah and there is none beside Me. I have given you the gentiles. For they will serve me and will be a treasure in this earth. I will establish all their goings. I will keep them in My ways, and I will be glorified.

A Place of Healing & Victory

" Trust in the LORD, and do good; Dwell in the land, and feed on His faithfulness." Psalm 37:3

Believe Me! Trust Me! I Am God and God alone! I have purposed to bring you into a place of healing and victory. I Am giving you a new perspective in Me! I will show you My ways and you will walk in them. From the beginning of time I have always had a people who sought Me and kept My ways. I will do no less in this hour! Seek Me! Trust Me! Rely on Me! I will never leave you or forsake you. I love you!

My Strength in Your Weakness

"My grace is sufficient for you, for My strength is made perfect in weakness." 2 Corinthians 12:9

My strength is made perfect in your weakness. I will cause you to overcome and you will rejoice before Me. Do not slumber nor sleep, but be sober and alert. I will give you the eye of an eagle that you may soar above your circumstances. That you may watch and pray with a discerning eye. I will move heaven and earth for My children, and I will do no less for you. For you are My child and I love you!

More Than a Conqueror

"Yet in all these things we are more than conquerors through Him who loved us." Romans 8:37

Trust Me as you walk your faith out. As you take the journey of life. It is true – Many are the afflictions of the righteous – But I the Lord delivers you from them all. I will deliver you! Troubles will come, but they will go and you will arise a victor. More than a conqueror. Abide in Me as I abide in you. Rely and trust in My promises. I will never fail you.. I have you in the palm of My hand. I will keep you and protect you. You will arise victorious in every area of your life. Rejoice and sing, for I Am doing a great work in you and through you in this hour. Rejoice I say for you truly will rise and shine in this hour and nothing will hold you back from My blessings. I Am The Lord your God and I fail not!

Arise & Shine

"Arise, shine; For your light has come! And the glory of the LORD is risen upon you. 2 For behold, the darkness shall cover the earth, And deep darkness the people; But the LORD will arise over you, And His glory will be seen upon you." Isaiah 60:1,2

Arise my child and shine; for I will cause My glory to be seen in you and through you. Yes there is much darkness in this world. But My glory is shining bright. My glory has never faded or diminished. But the fullness of who I Am is being revealed in this earth as the waters cover the sea. Let Me shine through you. Let me pour out My love on the hurting nations. I hear the cry and the groaning of the people of the earth. Many have corrupted and perverted My word and have not been a reflection of Me. You must go and shine My light and expose the lies and the deceptions. Show them that I Am a loving God. A God who saves those who others have given up hope that they will ever be saved. I will never cease from reaching My hand to those who are lost. For I love them and I died for them. I gave My life blood that they may know that there is a true and living God who is there for them. Yes, I AM that I AM and every device and scheme of the devil will not succeed. I have already determined the outcome. Join Me as I unfold my marvelous plans and show forth My glory in this hour. I sent the former rain but now I Am pouring out the latter rain. I will wash and cleanse the earth and many will know that I Am God. Many will be saved and many will populate heaven as I rescue them from the snares of sin and degradation. My church will arise in this hour. So arise My child and shine for your light has come.

I Am Your Treasure

"For where your treasure is, there your heart will be also."
Matthew 6:21

The treasure of your heart will always be Me, I will not allow the enemy to deceive you and to take you out of My hand. I have placed you securely in the palm of My hand. Learn to delight in me and all My ways. I will fill you every day with My goodness. Whatever you do – do it with all you have to Me. I will bless the work of your hands and give you favor. Do not fret over those who do not respond to My call. If they reject Me they will reject you. Pray for them and entrust them into My care. I Am God and there is no other.

I Will Build My Church

"I will build My church, and the gates of Hades shall not prevail against it." Matthew 16:18

I Am building My purposes in you. I Am giving you purpose and direction. Only look to Me. Seek My face. Search My Word. Hunger and thirst for My righteousness. Delight yourself in Me. I desire to bring in a harvest of souls into My kingdom over the next 2 months. Pray. Seek My face. Be obedient and I will move sovereignly, just as I promised. I will build My church! Just be a yielded vessel in My hand. There will be joy in My house in the days to come. Shout for joy! Sing praises to My name. Rejoice continually before Me. I Am the Rock of your salvation. Your buckler, shield and your high tower. The hope of all mankind.

Prepare the Net

"And He said to them, "Cast the net on the right side of the boat, and you will find some." John 21:6

I Am giving you a new beginning. Look to Me as your source. I Am your strength. I forgive iniquities. I Am a merciful God. Renew your strength. Walk uprightly and I will direct your pathways. I love you with an everlasting love. I will give you the tongue of the learned, and you will speak My word. Lives will be changed. Rejoice for this is the finest hour for My people. The harvest is ready for the ingathering of souls. Those who prepare their net will be ready. You do not have to fish all night and catch nothing. If you obey Me, you will know the heart of the Father and you will know where to cast your net. Prepare the net and prepare your heart for I Am coming soon in all of My glory. You will see Me face to face. Delight yourself in Me. I will satisfy your soul with good things. Only seek first the kingdom of God and My righteousness and I will add all things to you.

I Am With You

"I am with you always, even to the end of the age." Matthew 28:20

My Word will instruct you in all My ways. I will give purpose and direction. I will lead you by My Spirit. I will send you to places where I want to move through you. I Am making a way for you. I will provide. I will abide in you. With My hand of mercy I will keep you in all of My ways. Do not fret, for I Am with you always.

I Delight In You

"As for the saints who are on the earth, They are the excellent ones, in whom is all my delight." Psalm 16:3

Bring your offerings of praise to Me. I inhabit the praises of My people. I delight in a heart that honors and reveres My name. I love when a person chooses to love Me because they want to and not because they have to. Freely I have given to you, now freely give back. Your choice to walk with Me, to honor Me, to worship Me has been the joy of My heart. For I delight in you. I delight in the godly choices you have made. Do not be distracted by the inferior experiences the world has to offer you.. Come up here, come up now and experience the fullness of My love. Walk with Me and know I Am God. There is no other.

I Have Specific Plans For You

"For I know the thoughts that I think toward you, says the LORD, thoughts of peace and not of evil, to give you a future and a hope." Jeremiah 29:11

Draw near to Me. Do not let the distractions of this life pull you in a direction I have not sent you or led you. I have specific plans for you. There are many good things that you could be doing, but only do those things I have called you to. I Am your rock and your strength. I will supply all your need. I Am with you always. Make straight your path. Fix your eyes on Me and prosper and be blessed.

I Do Not Change

"Jesus Christ is the same yesterday, today, and forever."
Hebrews 13:8

I Am unchangeable. I Am the same yesterday, today and forever. That does not mean that I Am unwilling to move or withholding and stubborn. It means that who I Am does not change. My ability does not change. Circumstances in this life in the realm of time, does not affect or restrain Me from My plans for you and the earth. I will continue to forge My plans through My people. Many will know that I Am God and will be transformed for My glory. Reach out your hands to the lost. For when you do, I Am extending my hands through you. I will touch through you and I will fill My people with good things. Walk in obedience to My word and My ways and you will prosper in the things I have allowed in your life. Rejoice and be content in me. Circumstances change. People come and go. But I never change. I Am your solid rock and I Am a sure foundation.

Sing A Song To Me

"Sing praises to God, sing praises! Sing praises to our King, sing praises!" Psalm 47:6

My love for you is never ending, My love for you is true. My love for you brings singing, for My love for you is true. Lift your eyes and behold your bridegroom. Lift your eyes and behold your King. Sing a song of love and mercy. Sing a song to Me. For I have been with you in the night hours. I have comforted you with My love. Know that My love extends to you and that My mercy endures forever.

The Plans of My Heart

"The counsel of the LORD stands forever, The plans of His heart to all generations." Psalm 33:11

My light is shining in the darkness. My light will illumine your pathway that you will be able to see the plans I have for you. Do not fret and do not be dismayed, for I Am at work revealing My glory in this hour. I Am at work transforming lives. I will move through you to bring My Kingdom purposes to pass. I will expose every device and scheme of your enemy and I will make you victorious. So listen and obey. Follow and give Me praise. For I Am that I Am that I Am and there is no other. I Am the Great I Am and there is no other.

Drink From The Fountain

" Therefore with joy you will draw water from the wells of salvation." Isaiah 12:3

No other, No other. I Am your God. I will infuse your life with renewed strength for the journey ahead. Eat of My Word and be strengthened by the power of My Spirit. My life will infuse your life. I will transform and renew. So draw from the wells of salvation. Drink from the fountain of life. Draw near to the living water that flows from My throne to you. Drink deep and find your satisfaction in Me.

Draw Near To Me

"Draw near to God and He will draw near to you."
James 4:8

Draw near to Me. For I Am that I Am and I change not. I change all things for My purposes and glory, but I change not. I Am bringing you into a season of blessings and favor. This season is for the purpose of advancing my purposes. Rejoice and know that I have found a desire in you to touch lives for My glory. To see lives, churches and cities transformed. I will use you in this hour to reveal My love to people who serve Me out of fear, but do not serve Me out of love. I will make you an example of My love that others would experience my touch and embrace. I love you and I love My creation. I want to embrace you and the ones you touch with My unfailing love. Receive My touch in this hour. Receive My embrace in this hour. Receive a baptism of my love in this hour.

Dwell In My House

"One thing I have desired of the LORD, That will I seek: That I may dwell in the house of the LORD. All the days of my life." Psalm 27:4

Dwell in My house. Abide in my love. Do not let the distractions of this life keep you from living in My presence. I have prepared a place for you in this hour to abide in My love and My peace. You do not have to let the cares of this world rob you from all that I Am and all that I desire to give you. Dwell in my house. Live in My presence and be filled with all the fullness of who I Am. I love you, I love you, I love you. I Am with you always even to the end of this age.

I Make All Things New

"Behold, I make all things new." Revelation 21:5

Nothing will be impossible to those who trust Me. I will transform and renew your life everyday as you yield to Me and My purposes. Look to Me and receive My gift of love. My gift of faith. I will saturate your life and fill you with the treasures of heaven. I make all things new. This day I Am renewing your strength and renewing your vision. I will surround you with a hedge of My glory and provision. Everywhere you turn, you will see My hand at work on your behalf. You will walk in My favor. I decree it and who can reverse it? Take steps forward and walk through the doors I open for you. I Am bringing you to a place in me that will touch lives for My kingdom. The joy of bringing My harvest to Me will be your song daily and the joy of your heart.

Trust In Me With All Your Heart

"Trust in the LORD with all your heart, And lean not on your own understanding; In all your ways acknowledge Him, And He shall direct your paths". Proverbs 3:5,6

Trust in Me! Do not worry about what you see. Do not lean on your own understanding. But trust in Me. Acknowledge who I Am. I have the ability to change all things. My timing is always perfect. I will lead and guide you in this hour. Endure hardness as a good soldier. Do not run and try to escape. Stand still and see the salvation of your God. Hold the ground I have given you and taught you to dwell upon. Do not stumble or lose your footing in this hour. Look up to Me. Fix your eyes on Me. I will carry you through. I will!

Today is a Good Day

"This is the day the LORD has made; We will rejoice and be glad in it." Psalm 118:24

Today is a good day. A day to worship. A day to praise. A day to magnify My name. Look to Me and know that I Am at work in you. I will strengthen you in this hour. I will make your paths straight. Look to Me and know that I Am God. Put your trust in Me. I open doors and I shut doors. Trust Me that I will take you to where I want you. I will supply all your need. I will provide all that you need. I will fill you with good things that will overflow with My presence and My glory. Open your mouth wide and I will fill it.

Yes, Today is a Good Day

"Surely it is coming, and it shall be done, says the Lord GOD. "This is the day of which I have spoken." Ezekiel 39:8

Today is a good day, for I have formed and created my purposes for this day. I will make major shifts in regions around the world today. I will change and affect governments and will remove walls that have been put up to hinder My Gospel and My servants. Yes, today is a good day, for history will show that this date major changes took place around the world. Keep your eyes on Me, for I know the things that have been done in secret and I will expose those things. Get ready for an outpouring of My love, of My Spirit. You will receive new strength to rise up and fulfill your call and destiny. Look to Me and no other. I open doors and I shut doors. This day I open doors for you and you will walk through in victory carrying the banner I have placed in your hands. Prepare the way of the Lord!

My Light is Shining in The Darkness

"Arise, shine; For your light has come! And the glory of the LORD is risen upon you. 2 For behold, the darkness shall cover the earth, And deep darkness the people; But the LORD will arise over you, And His glory will be seen upon you." Isaiah 60:1,2

The light of My Gospel will set the captives free. My light is shining in the darkness. I will dispel the darkness with My love and My power. I will fill My servants with a determination to break through the barriers that stand before them. Rise up in My strength. Rise up in My power. I will transform your heart that you may serve Me with everything you have. I love you. Receive My love. You are chosen and called to be a spokesman in this hour. Speak forth with all that I have placed within you. You are My chosen. Let My light shine bright through you. Let My light fill you. Then your heart will be encouraged. Do not fear the darkness, for greater is He that is in you than he that is in the world.

Can You See Me Now?

"In the year that King Uzziah died, I saw the Lord sitting on a throne, high and lifted up, and the train of His robe filled the temple." Isaiah 6:1

Sometimes things have to change before you will see Me for who I Am. Your eyes have been fixed on others . This is the time for you to take your focus off of others and to put them on Me. I Am the author and the finisher of your faith. I will do more for you than you know how to ask Me for. I will remove those things that hinder so you can be totally free to follow Me. Can you see Me now?

Bring Your Offering

"Give to the LORD the glory due His name; Bring an offering, and come into His courts." Psalm 96:8

Bring your offering to Me. Let it be from a heart of worship and not out of obligation. For I desire that you would love Me because you choose to and not because it is the right thing to do. I have called you to myself. I have chosen you for My glory. Be filled with My Spirit. Be filled with My love. Walk according to My will and My way and you will be prosperous. You will be blessed. Serve Me with all your heart. Serve Me this day and I will unfold My manifold wisdom to you and you will walk in high places with sure steps. Walk with Me and listen to My heartbeat for the nations. I will move through you. I will fill you with My Spirit. Rejoice for I have all things in My hand. I will fill you every day with purpose and direction. I will fill you every day with wisdom and truth. You will walk uprightly in My love and My ways. You will walk according to My word. So lay your heart before Me this day and do not give your heart to another. I desire that you would give of yourself as a freewill offering to Me. Come to Me and lay at My feet as I speak to you in this hour. There are so many people and things requiring your attention . But I ask you to give Me your first fruits. Your best fruits of your day to Me. Do not give Me your leftovers. Many do this to Me and then believe they have done their duty in their relationship with Me. But am I not more than just an obligation? Am I not more than just a religious duty? Bring your offering to Me. Bring yourself to Me. Obedience is better than sacrifice.

Let The Redeemed Say So

"Let the redeemed of the LORD say so, whom He has redeemed from the hand of the enemy." Psalm 107:2

Rejoice and be glad! Lift your heart in song. Let the redeemed of the Lord say so!. My Spirit is moving in all the earth. Transforming, renewing and filling My people afresh and anew. I Am removing those things that hinder and I Am bringing forth My mighty miracles and blessings. Receive all that I have for you. Receive My hand of grace and mercy. Receive My love. I will bring correction where correction is needed. I will lovingly lead you into all truth for My name sake, my glory and your good. Receive My love. Receive My touch this very hour

I Know My Plans For You

"For I know the thoughts that I think toward you, says the LORD, thoughts of peace and not of evil, to give you a future and a hope." Jeremiah 29:11

Trust in Me and know that I work all things together for good. Do not be disheartened but rejoice in Me. For I know the plans I have for you. Plans to prosper you. Plans to bless you, that you may have hope and an expected end.. I will lead you all the days of your life. I will fill you with My Spirit.. Walk uprightly. Walk in My love. Do not be dismayed for I Am with you. I will open doors, and I will shut doors. You will know that I Am God. Nothing is impossible. Trust in Me and know that My hand of grace and mercy covers you.

More Than a Conqueror

"Yet in all these things we are more than conquerors through Him who loved us." Romans 8:37

I have taken you out of darkness and I have filled you with My light and My goodness. Love fills your heart. I have made you more than a conqueror. You are My child, and I will raise you up to walk in high places. You have been chosen to speak my heart, my words to a perverse generation. I will fill you with light and life. I will fill you with My love. Walk with Me and receive all that I have for you.. I will fill you daily. I will fill you with truth, My light, My love. You will walk in high places in Me. I will make a way where there seems to be no way. Watch Me as I unfold My plan for you. I will show you the path of life and in My presence there is fullness of joy. I will raise you up in this hour. You will see glorious things take place before your eyes. I Am a miracle working God. I have chosen you that I may be glorified in you and through you. Rejoice! This is a great hour! Now is the time. Now is the time.

Trust in The Lord

"It is better to trust in the LORD Than to put confidence in man." Psalm 118:8

Trust Me, I know what I Am doing.

I Work All Things Together

"And we know that all things work together for good to those who love God, to those who are the called according to His purpose" Romans 8:28

My Word is a lamp unto your feet and a light unto your pathway. I have chosen you in this hour to speak for Me. Let me flow through you like a river. Let Me move through you by My great love and power. Look to Me and know that I Am God. I will fill you. I will release you into My fullness. Rejoice in Me and know that I always work all things together for your good and My glory. Trust Me and know that nothing is impossible for Me. I make all things new in this hour. All things. I Am the God of new beginnings. I make all things new.

Fix Your Eyes on Me

" looking unto Jesus, the author and finisher of our faith.." Hebrews 12:2

Today I Am giving you My strength. Press forward and walk in My power. Delight yourself in Me. I will take you to greater heights in Me. Look not to your left or right, but fix your eye on Me. Fix your heart on Me. Bring Me your offerings and lay them at My feet. I will lift them up as sweet incense before Me. The fragrance of worship before My throne. Sing a new song. A song of victory. A song of joy. A song of praise. I will open the floodgates and pour out My abundant blessings. Receive My love. Receive My touch. Be transformed and be all that I have made you to be. I Am your God and your strength forever.

New things I Declare

" Behold, the former things have come to pass, And new things I declare; Before they spring forth I tell you of them." Isaiah 42:9

My child, trust in Me. Delight in Me. I will bring to pass all that I have promised. I will bless those who bless you, and curse those who curse you. I will release My abundance in your life. I Am preparing you in this hour. I Am bringing you into a place of grace. Open your eyes and your heart and receive My abundant love. For I Am changing you and I will give you favor. I will bless you with abundance that it may overflow and bless others. This day I will open a door of blessing that will fill and flood your life. Receive My gift for it will sustain you in this hour. The harvest is great but the laborers are few. I Am sending you forth into My harvest fields. Go forth and bless the nations. I will fill your mouth and your heart. Rejoice. Rejoice the former things have come to pass and new things I declare to you.

Dwell in My House

" One thing I have desired of the LORD, That will I seek: That I may dwell in the house of the LORD All the days of my life, To behold the beauty of the LORD, And to inquire in His temple." Psalm 27:4

Dwell in My house. Seek my face. Do not be distracted by the cares and issues of life. Fix your eyes on Me. See Me in all of my glory and beauty. Do not seek the treasures of this world. They are not lasting but they falter and fall by the wayside. But I Am from everlasting to everlasting. I Am God. I Am the treasure that you seek. Receive Me now!

My Grace is Sufficient

"My grace is sufficient for you, for My strength is made perfect in weakness." 2 Corinthians 12:9

My child, My strength is made perfect in your weakness. I Am sending you as My ambassador of love. Let My love be poured out through you. Let My joy be poured out through you. I want you to reflect My character in all you do. Let My light shine through you. I will fill you every day with My Spirit. Rejoice and be glad, for I Am with you in Spirit and in truth. Sing the song of the redeemed. Sing the song of joy and walk with Me. My hand has been on you and I will prosper you. I will take you to My high places and bless you. I Am with you. Listen for My voice. Do not allow frustrations to steal your song and your joy. Always look to Me, the author and finisher of your faith.

My Treasure in You

" But we have this treasure in earthen vessels , that the excellence of the power may be of God and not of us." 2 Corinthians 4:7

My strength is made perfect in your weakness. My desire for you is that you be filled with all the fullness of My power. That you move and operate in My strength. For I have placed My treasure in your earthen vessel. I Am the source of everything that is true and righteous. Walk in My love and be saturated by My Spirit. Receive the blessings I promised to all those who are descendants of Abraham. I make all things new. Every plan and device of your enemy will fall apart, for I Am with you to bless you. And bless you, I will indeed!

Better is One Day in My Courts

" Better is one day in your courts than a thousand elsewhere.." Psalm 84:10 NIV

Delight yourself in Me. Keep your focus on My kingdom matters. For a day in my courts is worth more than a thousand days elsewhere. My Spirit is leading you and My love is guiding you. Always walk in love and you will never fail. For love never fails. Sing a new song. Sing a song of victory. A song of praise and restoration. I Am your treasure and your pearl of great price. I have chosen you for such a time as this. I have given you My Spirit. I Am filling you every day and every hour. Do not strive or stress. I order the steps of the righteous and My hand is upon you to bless you and to keep you in all of My ways.

I Will Light Your Path

"Your word is a lamp to my feet And a light to my path." Psalm 119:105

Go forward and I will shine My light on your path. Rejoice in Me. Bring your sacrifice of praise. My ways are far above your ways. So come up higher. Do not judge or make decisions based on what you see or what you are experiencing at this present time. Begin to prepare and make ready for what I Am about to do and what I have promised to do. Get ready for the ride of your life as I propel you forward to advance My Kingdom. I am creating divine appointments where I Am sending you. Be ready, for the latter will be greater than the former.

Nothing Is Impossible

"With men this is impossible, but with God all things are possible." Matthew 19:26

Nothing will be impossible to those who believe. My Spirit is at work in you. Transforming and renewing all that I desire to accomplish in you. You will be a royal diadem reflecting and showing forth My glory. Look to Me and no other, for I Am your strength, hope and salvation. Bring an offering to Me of praise. Lift up your voice in song and rejoice. I Am the rock of your salvation. Put your trust in Me. Put your hope in Me. I Am bringing you to a place of victory where you will rise in My strength and overcome every obstacle that stands in your way. I Am filling you this day with a renewed power and strength. Walk uprightly. Keep your eyes and attention on Me. I will never leave you or forsake you. I will never let you falter or fail. You are more than a conqueror. I Am walking in the midst of the candlesticks. I have ignited the passion of love in your heart. I will pour My love through you. Open your mouth wide and I will fill it. I will fill your life with good things. You will prosper in My kingdom purposes. I Am your rock and salvation. The God in whom you trust. The I Am. I will perform My word that I have spoken and you will be blessed.

I Work All Things For Your Good

" And we know that in all things God works for the good of those who love him, who have been called according to his purpose." Romans 8:28

Do you believe I Am working everything together for your good? I Am!

I Will Shine Through You

"You are the light of the world." Matthew 5:14

Bring an offering of praise to me. Show forth My glory in the earth. You are a diamond in My crown that reflects my light and glory. I have faceted you that others would see my multifaceted reflection of who I Am. The diamond in itself does not possess the light and glory, but reflects it. I have formed you and created you to be able to reflect My light and glory.. Of yourself you can do nothing in the absence of My light and glory. So present yourself in My presence and let Me shine through you that My kingdom would be established in all you say and do for My glory.

Ambassadors

" Now then, we are ambassadors for Christ, as though God were pleading through us: we implore you on Christ's behalf, be reconciled to God." 2 Corinthians 5:20

I have called you. I have chosen you. I Am sending you. I have made you an ambassador for My kingdom. Sing and rejoice, for the time has come to touch the nations. I will use you for My glory. Lives will be changed. I will have My way. That which I declared will come to pass and nothing can or will hinder My purposes. I love you and I have chosen you for My glory. Walk in the fullness of My Spirit. I will transform lives through you. I love you. You are the apple of My eye and the joy of My heart

No Condemnation

"There is therefore now no condemnation to those who are in Christ Jesus.." Romans 8:1

Today is a new day. Rejoice in Me. For I Am your inheritance. The things of this world are passing. They are corruptible. I Am with you always and I Am incorruptible. So cling to Me and know that you are rich with the glory of My kingdom. My kingdom will have no end. My riches are boundless. Keep your mind, your eyes and your heart fixed on Me. I Am your treasure and your pearl of great price. I love you. Do not walk or live in condemnation. But walk in Me and My love. Know that I Am for you and not against you.

My Divine Nature

"by which have been given to us exceedingly great and precious promises, that through these you may be partakers of the divine nature.." 2 Peter 1:4

Trust in Me. I will never fail. My ways are so far above your ways. Know that I love you and that I will supply all your need. I bring you into the fullness of My blessings every day. Reach out and be a partaker of My divine nature. Clothe yourself in My love, mercy and grace. I will adorn you with My nature. Clothe yourself in righteousness. Clothe yourself in my truth. I Am making you a glorious representation of My character. Let My presence fill you and My light infuse you that others will see Christ in you, the hope of glory. The Light of the World. The Bright and Morning Star.

Do Not Worry

"Don't worry about anything; instead, pray about everything; tell God your needs, and don't forget to thank him for his answers" Philippians 4:6. TLB

Do not worry or fret, for I Am greater than any problem in this life. Nothing is too difficult for Me. Place the issues of this life in my hands and trust Me to do a great work. I will renew your mind and your strength. I will fill you with truth, light and understanding. Walk with Me. Know that I Am God. Every day is a new opportunity to walk with Me and to draw near to Me. I have formed you and made you after My heart and image. Shine your light. Shine it bright. Know that I will pour My love through you. Lives will be changed. Cities and nations transformed by the power of My Spirit. Rejoice for this is a great hour when I Am pouring out My Spirit on all flesh. I will open doors for you. I will supply your every need. Let Me build through you. I will lay a foundation and I will build on that foundation. When the building is complete then your journey on this earth will be complete. Keep building with Me and I will unfold My plan before you. I love you and have great plans for you. Get your heart ready. Prepare. Dig ditches. For I am moving throughout the earth and those who are prepared will experience a mighty harvest of souls into My kingdom.

" If you wait for perfect conditions, you will never get anything done." Ecclesiastes 11:4 TLB

I Have Come To Give Life

"The thief does not come except to steal, and to kill, and to destroy. I have come that they may have life, and that they may have it more abundantly." John 10:10

Bring to Me your offering of praise. Let faith arise in your heart. This is an hour of restoration and healing for all things. The devourer has tried to steal, kill and destroy, but I have come to give life and that more abundantly. Behold I make all things new. I Am the repairer of the breach. I will heal and restore. The former will not outshine the latter. The latter will be greater than the former. So shine, shine, shine. Let My light shine. This year will be a year of great harvest and blessing in My kingdom. The time is at hand. The time is now. The harvest is now. Rise and work My fields. Work in My harvest and know that I Am God. Know that I Am gathering My people from the ends of the earth. I Am bringing them into My net of safety. Rescuing them from destruction. Put your hand in mine and follow Me. Place your feet in My footprints as I lead you forward in My purposes. You are the apple of My eye. Whoever touches you ,touches the apple of My eye. I Am releasing you into My perfect plan and purpose. I will anoint you to accomplish that which I have sent you to do. You will see a great harvest and many will come to know Me. Take My healing to the nations. Take My love to the hurting. I will be glorified in the earth.

" Those from among you shall build the old waste places;
You shall raise up the foundations of many generations;
And you shall be called the Repairer of the Breach,
The Restorer of Streets to Dwell In." Isaiah 58:12

My Word Will Never Fail

"Heaven and earth will pass away, but My words will by no means pass away." Matthew 24:35

My Word will never fail
The words of others will fail.
But I never fail.
I have the ability to keep My Word.
So why do you believe the words of others over My Word?
Let My Word have precedence over all other words.
I will bring to pass that which I have promised.
It may not be in the way you expect it.
But it will come to pass.
It will accomplish exactly what I have intended it to accomplish.

All Things Are Possible With Me

"The things which are impossible with men are possible with God." Luke 18:27

I Am making a way for you. Now is the time to trust Me and to rely on My Spirit and My Word. I have told you many times that nothing is impossible for Me. Now is the time to believe it. Confess those things from your mouth.
Out of the abundance of the heart the mouth speaks.
Speak truth!
Speak life!

Give Me Your Burdens

"Cast your burden on the LORD, And He shall sustain you; He shall never permit the righteous to be moved."
Psalm 55:22

Bring to Me your concerns, your burdens and know that I love you and that I have a solution to every problem. Do not fear that which could come upon you. I know the plans I have for you. Plans to prosper and to bless you. My purposes will be fulfilled in you and through you. Rejoice, for this is a day of blessing in the midst of failures and disappointments. Rejoice in Me. Rejoice in My love. Rejoice in My perfect plan for your life. Know that I Am God and all things are held upright by the power of My hand.

I Speak and it is Done

"Then God saw everything that He had made, and indeed it was very good." Genesis 1:31

I brought you out of darkness into My marvelous light. I put a new song in your mouth. My light will illuminate every part of your life. My Word will produce good fruit. I Am your deliverer. My ways and My plans are greater than any obstacle that may try to stand in your way. So look to Me and know that I Am God. There is hope in no other. I speak and it is done. All creation bows at My feet. All creation obeys My voice. I Am your rock and your strength and your portion forever.

From Glory to Glory

"But we all, with unveiled face, beholding as in a mirror the glory of the Lord, are being transformed into the same image from glory to glory, just as by the Spirit of the Lord." 2 Corinthians 3:18

New things will begin to spring forth in your life. I am changing you from glory to glory. Rejoice and know that I Am working in you a new measure of faith. That you may believe for the highest and best for your life. Do not worry about tomorrow. But look to me for direction and guidance. My Word will reveal new nuggets of truth to you in this hour. Allow the revelation of all that I Am to come to you and renew your thinking. I desire to bring you into a deeper revelation of all who I Am, that you can rise up to be who I have made you and called you to be. Rejoice, rejoice, rejoice. I Am coming to you in this hour to reveal My truths. Truths that will set you free and cause you to rise up. For I have many things for you to do. Do not waste time, for time is a commodity that I have given you that must be used for the highest and best of My kingdom. Look to Me for guidance and I will bring to pass those things that I have promised. Those things that I have willed to come to pass in your life. Look to Me for fresh revelation of all that I Am. For I Am that I Am.

Jesus said to them, "Most assuredly, I say to you, before Abraham was, I AM." John 8:58

Shine in the Darkness

"For behold, the darkness shall cover the earth, And deep darkness the people; But the LORD will arise over you, And His glory will be seen upon you." Isaiah 60:2

New things will begin to spring forth. You are My chosen, My child and I know you. Believe Me for greater things, knowing that the vast resources of heaven are yours to advance My kingdom. Know that I Am God and I Am looking for those who can believe Me for My highest and best. The revelation of all that I Am will carry you through the days ahead. My Word is a lamp unto your feet and a light unto your pathway. Sing the song of the redeemed. Sing the song of the conqueror. I have equipped you to overcome every obstacle. I Am bringing you into a season of miracles. Everyday My miracles will unfold. Your victory is secured in Me. My love will fill your heart and your life. I Am making you a praise in the earth. Many will be drawn to the light. Listen and be obedient. I have chosen you to shine My light bright in the darkness. Shine so that darkness will be exposed and dispelled. I Am sending an army of My Angels with many gifts to distribute. I Am looking for sons and daughters that will be carriers of My anointing. Who will deliver My gifts to a people that are scattered like sheep who have wandered far from the fold. I Am bringing them back to Me.
I Am sending you to bring them back to Me. I Am with you always. I will use you to touch many who are at a cross road. The time is now. Do not delay your obedience. I will make a way for you and you will be victorious in all that I send you to do.

I Have Betrothed You

"For I have betrothed you to one husband, that I may present you as a chaste virgin to Christ." 2 Corinthians 11:2

Bring Me your praise. Bring Me a heart of worship. Open your heart to Me and know I will bring My abiding presence. I desire to dwell in your midst. You are My chosen. You are My beloved. I have betrothed you to myself. Draw near to Me and listen. Do not be distracted. Do not look upon another for I Am your life. I Am your hope. I Am your love. I dwell in the midst of My people. Remember that I called you. I will equip you. I will fight your battles, for they are My battles also. I will work in a greater measure than you know how to ask Me for. I love you!

I Will Supply

"And my God shall supply all your need according to His riches in glory by Christ Jesus." Philippians 4:19

Nothing is impossible for those who believe-for nothing is impossible for God. I have brought you to this place for a season and now I Am taking you further in My plan for My glory. I will supply all your need. You do not have to fear. For I Am with you. I will bring you into My purposes as you put your trust in Me. Bring your desires, concerns and issues to Me - knowing I have the answers and solutions you need. I Am changing you for My glory and I Am renewing your strength and vision. I will do more for you than you know how to ask Me for. Rejoice, for this is an accelerated hour in My kingdom. I will multiply everything I put in your hands.

For Daily Living

New Things I Declare

"Behold, the former things have come to pass, And new things I declare; Before they spring forth I tell you of them." Isaiah 42:9

Listen to My voice. Know that I Am with you. My rod and My staff comfort you. Bring to Me your offering of praise. I delight in you My child. You are a treasure to Me. Know My love for you is everlasting. I will lead you and guide you by My Spirit. Trust in Me and know that I Am God. Know that I Am the Way, the Truth and the Life. I will bring you into the fullness of My Spirit and My will for your life. I Am sending you in My love and power. I will break the chains of the wicked. I will bring you into the fullness of all I have for you.. This is an hour to walk in the fullness of My Spirit. Rejoice for the former things have come to pass and new things I declare to you.

A Good Work In You

"Being confident of this very thing, that He who has begun a good work in you will complete it until the day of Jesus Christ." Philippians 1:6

You are on the threshold of a tremendous blessing. Open wide-prepare to receive. For I will pour it forth with abundance and blessing. Like a waterfall I will pour out My Spirit. The anointing will increase. I Am changing you. You will not remain the same. Have I not been faithful to bring increase? I will bring increase in you. Rejoice for I Am working in you producing My purposes in and through you. Rejoice for I have begun a good work in you and I will continue to perform it.

Times and Seasons are Changing

"Do not remember the former things, Nor consider the things of old. 19 Behold, I will do a new thing, Now it shall spring forth; Shall you not know it? I will even make a road in the wilderness And rivers in the desert." Isaiah 43:18,19

New things I declare to you. New things. I Am changing you and bringing you into My fullness. Rejoice and know that times and seasons are changing. I Am accelerating My kingdom purposes in the earth. A great harvest is at hand. I Am looking, seeking and desiring those who are willing to be obedient. To see a mighty outpouring upon the earth. A torrential rain is coming that will drench My people with the power of My Spirit. It will literally wash away the stench of this world and bring a mighty transformation. I Am raising up a generation that will go forth as an army. Ready and equipped for battle. Ready to be obedient to My every command. I will bless such a people with My love and blessing. Signs and wonders in the earth. Signs of My coming. My imminent return. Work while it is day. Work while you have breath on the earth. Each day is a gift and a treasure from above. Cherish it and use it for My glory.

Your God Reigns

"Be renewed in the spirit of your mind." Ephesians 4:23

I will transform and renew your mind. I will make you a vessel fully yielded to My power and glory. My love for you will never end. I Am with you always. I will take you from glory to glory. I will turn all things around for you. I will open doors. I will bless and prosper you in My ways. So rejoice, receive and remind yourself that your God reigns!

I Will Direct Your Steps

*"The steps of a good man are ordered by the LORD,
And He delights in his way." Psalm 37:23*

This is the beginning of great things to come. I Am making a way for you. I will reveal and show you things to come, all for My glory- all for My purposes. I Am enlarging your ministry. I Am opening doors of effectual service. I will put all things into perspective. I will cause My upright and righteous ways to be revealed. Trust in Me and know that I work all things together for good. I who formed you, shaped you and gave you My Spirit will enlarge your borders. I have called you to walk in high places. I have placed your feet for mY glory. I placed you where I chose and I will continue to order your steps. I will release My power to touch the nations. I will send you forth to bring great revival and the move of My Spirit. I will pour out My wisdom and knowledge in you and through you. This is My finest hour. This is the hour of victory. This is My season and time that the Bride of Christ will be adorned, honored and displayed for the world to see her beauty and demeanor. As the world looks upon My people – they will be drawn to Me. I have chosen many in this hour. Signs and wonders will be manifest and many lives will be transformed in these last days. A great harvest awaits for the ingathering. I Am raising up in this hour a people who will go in obedience to My commands. Go – for the harvest is great, but the laborers are few. Go- for there are many whose lives are weighing in the balance. Go- in My love and in My strength – GO!

My Ways Above Your Ways

"For as the heavens are higher than the earth, So are My ways higher than your ways, And My thoughts than your thoughts.
Isaiah 55:9

Do nothing without My guidance. Listen carefully to My voice and step out in faith. I will make your path clearer everyday Others may try to stop you. Other may not understand – but you listen to Me and you will experience the miraculous. My ways are so far above your ways. Draw near to Me and learn of My ways and you will find life. Abundant life. The treasures of heaven. The fountain of grace. The river of My love and more. For the glories of heaven and of My kingdom cannot be exhausted. I will cause you to live in my abundant overflow daily. Open wide and receive my blessings this day.

The Abundance of Your Heart

"For out of the abundance of the heart the mouth speaks."
Matthew 12:34

Walk with Me and know that I will fight your battles. I will fight for you. Rest and trust in Me. For is there anything to hard for Me? I will draw you nearer to Me every day. So praise Me with your whole heart. Praise Me every day and always. Let the song of the redeemed rise within you. Let My praises rise on your lips. For out of the abundance of your heart your mouth will speak. Let Me dwell in you abundantly. A never ending fountain that will continually flow and never run dry. Never run dry.

Do Not Fear Your Enemy

"And do not fear those who kill the body but cannot kill the soul." Matthew 10:28

Bring everything to me. Bring all the issues of life and know that I have the power to change all things. I love you. I will care for you and protect you. Do not fear what the enemy can do – for Am I not greater than anything and anyone who would try to stand in your way? Trust Me and know that I Am that I Am. I give strength to the weak. I uphold all things by My hand. My hand of grace and mercy will secure you in this hour. Trust Me and know that I Am God.

Draw Near To Me

"Draw near to God and He will draw near to you." James 4:8

My light will shine in the darkness. I will lift you on the wings of an eagle. I will bring you into My presence, surround you with My grace and renew your strength. Delight yourself in Me. Sing songs of worship. For I inhabit your praises and fill you with good things. Draw near to Me and I will draw near to you. I will surround you with My love and securely hold you within My plans for you. Nothing will stop Me from keeping you in the palms of My hands- holding you through every storm of life.

Bear Much Fruit

"By this My Father is glorified, that you bear much fruit; so you will be My disciples." John 15:8

Draw near to Me. I have chosen you. I have called you and I will bring you into My presence. With joy you will rise in My presence. You will rise in My love. I will speak to you in love and will fill you with good things. I have chosen you to go forth and bear much fruit. Do not be afraid and do not be dismayed, for I Am with you. I will move through you to produce My kingdom purposes in the earth. Sing! Shout! Rejoice and know that I Am God. Know that I Am that I Am. Unfolding my blessings from generation to generation. Doing wonders to all nations. Transforming lives for eternity. I Am God and there is no other.

The Victory Is Yours

"But thanks be to God, who gives us the victory through our Lord Jesus Christ." 1 Corinthians 15:57

The victory is yours and always. I have never left you and I never will. I secured the victory for you a long time ago. What I have done and completed cannot and will not be reversed. I have made you more than a conqueror. So stand still. Rest in Me and know that I have already secured the victory. I will manifest it in this hour. Wait on Me and do not waver in your faith. But trust that I know what I Am doing!

I Am For You – Not Against You

"If God is for us, who can be against us?" Romans 8:31

Receive My love. Receive My blessings. Know that I Am for you and not against you. I Am bringing you into the fullness of My Spirit that you may walk in my love and mercy. I will renew your mind and bring you to a place of victory in Me. I have called you and I will bless you as you step out in obedience. I Am making a way for you. I Am bringing about My purposes in you and through you. Know that I Am God and My ways are righteous. My truths are everlasting and unfailing. I will bring to pass that which I have ordained – in this hour – in this season. Rejoice for the former and latter rain are merging and a downpour of all that I Am will saturate your soul. I will bring to pass My great plans that I have spoken about in My word. You will know that nothing shall be impossible to those who believe and follow Me in obedience. I Am your rock and strength and your portion forever.

Fix You Eyes On Me

"looking unto Jesus, the author and finisher of our faith.."
Hebrews 12:2

Fix your eyes on Me! Do not be distracted by the cares of this world. I Am your God and your strength. Look deep into my eyes of love and know that I will never allow you to be snared by your enemies. I Am your solid rock and your sure foundation. Plant your feet and do not be moved. Fine tune your hearing to only hear that which I Am speaking to you in this hour. I will hide you under the shadow of my wings forever. That which I have begun – I will complete in you.

I Have Chosen You

"For many are called, but few are chosen." Matthew 22:14

Delight yourself in Me and receive the treasures of heaven. Know this – that I have chosen you. That I have given you My love and mercy. You will rise in this hour. You will walk in My love. For I have called you to myself. I have put My Spirit in you so that you would be a blessing in the earth and a catalyst for revival. Many are called but few are chosen. I chose you because you have yielded your heart to Me. Because you desire to please and honor Me. I Am bringing you into a new season. A season of blessing. Do not doubt and do not fear. I have always been faithful to bring you into My highest and best. Keep your eyes focused on Me. Keep your eyes focused on My word and on My purposes. I Am your God and your strength. Delight yourself in Me. I Am your rock and your song. Sing of My love and rejoice in My grace and mercy. For My love endures forever.

Dance With Me

"And a time to dance;.." Ecclesiastes 3:4

Rise up and dance with Me. This is the time to dance. It doesn't matter if things appear to be going good or bad. I still love you and I have never let go of you. So run into My embrace and dance with Me. You will forget your problems. You will forget your enemies. You will forget what it was that you were worrying about. Instead you will be lost in My embrace and My everlasting love. Come dance with Me!

Let Me Search Your Heart

"O LORD, You have searched me and known me." Psalm 139:1

I Am working in you and through you. I Am changing you. Delight in Me and walk in the fullness of what I have for you. My word will guide you. I will fill you with My power and anointing. Bring Me your heart. Let Me search every part. I will transform you to rise and fulfill My call and purpose in your life. Give your praise to Me. Shout aloud with joy. Rejoice in My kingdom purposes. My Spirit is flowing like a torrential river. Nothing will be able to stand in the way of My purposes. The dam has broken and this is the hour of My great outpouring.

I Speak and it is Done

"God, who gives life to the dead and calls those things which do not exist as though they did;" Romans 4:17

Bring your sacrifice of praise and worship. Bring your song of worship. I Am the Lord. I call those things that are not as though they are. For I speak and it is done. I spoke the worlds into existence. I created all things. I will speak and create in you all that I have determined. You will walk in victory. My strength is made perfect in your weakness. Trust in Me and know that I Am God. I call from the north, south , east and west. I bring My sons and daughters from afar. I will bring my blessings to you. Begin to see those things that don't exist as though they exist. For I will speak and it will be done. I Am the creator of all things and I will produce in you those things that I have determined for you. My word will never fail. Do not be swayed by the things you see in the natural. I Am supernatural and nothing is impossible for Me!

The Word of My Power

"..upholding all things by the word of His power,..."
Hebrews 1:3

Draw near to Me. Trust in Me, for I Am you rock and your strength. I have set in motion My plans and no one can stop Me. That which I have ordained will come to pass. Rejoice in My love. Rejoice in My Word. Sing praise and lift up My name in all the earth. As I Am glorified you will see transformation take place in every environment. I created all things and I hold all things together by the word of My power. I will bring order where there has been scattering. I will bring purpose where there has been doubt and confusion. I will establish My kingdom purposes. Walk with Me and I will remove every obstacle that stands in your way. Receive MY blessings and My anointing in this hour. Receive My love and be saturated in My presence.

You Are Not Alone

"I am with you always, even to the end of the age."
Matthew 28:20

Do you feel alone? I have never left you. Others may leave. Others may forsake you. But I will never leave you. You are not alone. Stop right now. I Am speaking to you. I love you with an everlasting love. My love is not based on your performance. I love you right now and right where you are at. Take My hand and walk with me. I will take you out of this circumstance and you will come forth victorious. Receive the security of My love and embrace in this hour.

For Daily Living

A Song In The Night

"I call to remembrance my song in the night." Psalm 77:6

My Word will never fail. My Word abides forever. It is established in the heavens and manifest on earth. I will give you a song in the night. I will raise you up in this hour. Rejoice before Me. Sing songs of worship and praise. I will fill your life with good things. I will fill your heart with wisdom. That which looks impossible will be made possible as I move heaven and earth on your behalf. Look to Me. Trust in Me. I will open your eyes of understanding. Praise Me in the hard times and in the good times. I Am not moved by circumstances, but circumstances are moved by Me. I will remove every obstacle that stands in your way. You will rise in this hour and walk on the high places in Me. Keep your eyes focused on Me. Do not let the cares of this life sway you. I Am your solid rock foundation. I have established you in Me. Walk with Me and know that I Am God. I Am your rock and your strength. A fountain that will never run dry. I will bring a refreshing to you in this hour. Drink deep of the river of life. Drink deep and be satisfied in Me. I Am your high tower and shelter in the time of storms. Hide yourself in Me. Hide yourself in Me. Hide yourself in Me.

"For who is God, except the LORD? And who is a rock, except our God? 33 God is my strength and power, And He makes my way perfect. 34 He makes my feet like the feet of deer, And sets me on my high places." 2 Samuel 22: 32-35

The Enemy Cannot Stop You

"He who is in you is greater than he who is in the world."
1.John 4:4

Abide in Me as I abide in you. Look to Me for all things. I Am with you always. Delight yourself in Me. I will bring you to that place in Me that you will find rest, peace and My abiding presence. Do not think it strange the battle that has raged against you, trying to stop and hinder you. The enemy of your soul is fearful of what I can do through you. The enemy cannot stop you, because nothing can stop Me from that which I have purposed. I will give you favor in this hour. You will excel in my purposes. Rejoice for this is a victorious hour and season in your life. I will open doors of effectual service. Go forward in obedience and I will provide above and beyond you could ask or think. Sing a song of victory. Sing a song of love. Sing the song of the redeemed. Sing the song of heaven. I will come to you and refresh you in this hour. I Am God and there is no other. There is no other. There is no other. I Am faithful and I will bring to pass all that I have promised in your life.

Be Healed

"For I am the LORD who heals you." Exodus 15:26

I want to heal you now. Don't wait until tomorrow. I want to touch you now. Let me touch your heart. Let me embrace you in My love. My love is a healing balm. You have been wounded, hurt and abused, but I want to heal you. Will you let me? Receive My touch right now. I Am removing the pain and restoring your joy! I Am your love and strength forever.

Do You Know I Love You?

"Yes, I have loved you with an everlasting love; Therefore with lovingkindness I have drawn you." Jeremiah 31:3

Do you know I love you? Do you know I love you with an everlasting love? I have given you My Spirit in full measure. I have not withheld My love. I have lavishly poured out My love upon you. Receive My great love. Know that I Am with you always. I am with you even in the times when you feel like you are not being effective or productive in My kingdom. Know that I will remove those things that hinder you and stand in your way. I Am your deliverer. I Am your strength. Trust in Me. From this day forward look to Me for all things. Know that I will do more than you know how to ask Me for. I will take the little that I have placed in your hand and multiply it over and over again. You will see miracles, signs and wonders. This is an hour of favor and breakthrough for you. Rejoice for I Am King. I Am gracious to My children. I will do more than an earthly father could do. I Am God and there is no other. There is no other.

You Can Trust Me

"Trust in the LORD with all your heart, And lean not on your own understanding." Proverbs 3:5

You can trust Me. Even when it seems like I have failed you – realize that I only failed your perception of what should have happened. But I know better and I know what is best for you. I will always work all things together for your good and for My glory. Believe Me when I say- "I know what I Am doing!"

Rejoice

"Rejoice in the Lord always. Again I will say, rejoice!"
Philippians 4:4

My strength is made perfect in your weakness. My light will shine in the darkness and will enlighten your path. Do not be afraid or dismayed, for I Am with you. Just look to Me for all things, for I will supply all things for My glory. You rejoice for I Am unfolding My plans in this hour. I Am unfolding My purposes in this hour. Rejoice for great is the mercy and grace that I have poured upon you. You will see in the coming months a release of favor on your behalf. You have been obedient to follow My leading. Now watch as I unfold my great plan for you in this hour. REJOICE!

Sacrifices of Joy

"Therefore I will offer sacrifices of joy in His tabernacle;
I will sing, yes, I will sing praises to the LORD." Psalm 27:6

Trust in Me and do not let the cares of this world drag you down. I Am your sure foundation. Build your thoughts and desires on Me. I will never fail you. I will not fail to bring My purposes to pass. Sing praises just as they are sung in heaven. Enveloped in My love and constant care. Bring your sacrifices of joy as the divine exchange continually takes place. Enter into a higher plane of abiding in My lovingkindness. A place of surety and peace. Rejoice in Me knowing that I work all things together for your good and MY glory. Rejoice for this is a great hour in My kingdom. A great hour in your life and ministry. I Am guiding you by My Spirit. I love you with an everlasting love.

Pure Unconditional Love

"That Christ may dwell in your hearts through faith; that you, being rooted and grounded in love, 18 may be able to comprehend with all the saints what is the width and length and depth and height --19 to know the love of Christ which passes knowledge; that you may be filled with all the fullness of God." Ephesians 3:17-19

Remember always that I love you. My love for you is not based on your performance. But My love is a pure love, an unconditional love. My love is never ending. It cannot be destroyed. For I Am the very essence and embodiment of love. My greatest desire is that you would know and experience the depth, height, length and width of My love. That you would be filled with all My fullness. I Am for you and not against you. I will cause you to rise above your circumstances as you learn to abide in My love. Let faith arise. Let your heart not be troubled, but fully trust in My love and My ability to change and transform all things. I Am with you always. I will not reject you or destroy you. I Am building in you a sure foundation that cannot be shaken. I Am building in you a strong structure that will withstand every scheme, device and tactic of the enemy – the devil. Do not fear for it will backfire and fall apart on the devil. I always come out the victor and thus you become more than a conqueror always.

"And we have known and believed the love that God has for us. God is love, and he who abides in love abides in God, and God in him." 1 John 4:16

Sweet-Smelling Aroma

"Therefore be imitators of God as dear children.2 And walk in love, as Christ also has loved us and given Himself for us, an offering and a sacrifice to God for a sweet-smelling aroma." Ephesians 5:1,2

Bring to Me your offerings and lay them at My feet. I will receive them as a sweet incense rising before Me. An aroma of the true reflection of your heart. I will search you and sift you and reveal the true motives of your heart. I do not do this to shame you –but instead to change you. I desire to lift you to a higher spiritual plane in Me. A place where you will walk in victory. A place where fruitfulness is a natural outgrowth of your life. I have appointed you. I have chosen you and I delight in you. Let confidence arise in your heart so that you can stand and boldly proclaim My Word. My Word is life giving and life changing. My Word will cleanse, deliver and heal. Let Me open the floodgates. Let Me pour out My Spirit in and through you. Worship Me in the beauty of holiness. I will take you higher and higher in Me. Arise and shine – this is the greatest hour for the church to arise. Arise I say –Arise!

Behind The Veil

"This hope we have as an anchor of the soul, both sure and steadfast, and which enters the Presence behind the veil." Hebrews 6:19

My presence is everywhere. Many never experience My manifest presence. I have manifested myself to you in many situations and places. But I invite you to come behind the veil into My presence. My intimate personal presence. COME!

Bring Your Offering

"8 Give to the LORD the glory due His name; Bring an offering, and come into His courts. 9 Oh, worship the LORD in the beauty of holiness!" Psalm 96:8,9

Bring your offering of praise and lay it at My feet. I will lift it up and receive it as a sweet incense before Me. I will cause it to be multiplied back to you in the abundance of My manifest presence and the release of My blessings into your hands. Sing, pray and worship. Let these things rise in strength in your life. I Am releasing My glory in the earth. I Am pouring My love on the nations. I will rescue the perishing from their evil ways. What the devil intended for evil I will turn for good. Get ready for a great harvest. I Am with you. I Am your God. Rejoice for this is the finest hour for My church – My people.

Show Forth My Love

"Do to others as you would have them do to you" Luke 6:31 NIV

Do unto others as you would have others do unto you. I search the hearts and I know those who are mine. As you show forth My love to others, I will show forth My love to you. Changes are coming. Changes that will propel you forward in My love. Do not be afraid for I Am with you. I will cause you to rise upon the wings like an eagle. Nothing will be impossible for those who believe. Nothing! Choose life – choose Me. Choose My will and My way. Choose blessings. I delight in you for you are truly the apple of My eye. The joy of My heart

My Word

*" So shall My word be that goes forth from My mouth;
It shall not return to Me void, But it shall accomplish what I please, And it shall prosper in the thing for which I sent it."
Isaiah 55:11*

My Word will light your path
My Word will transform your life.
My Word will fill you with truth, light and understanding.
My Word will set you free.
My Word will abide forever.
My Word will never fail.
Trust Me and know that My Word will never return void.
NEVER!
It will produce life & light where there has been death & darkness.
My Word has the power to transform all things.
I will change your heart.
I will change your life.
Be not afraid, draw near to Me.
I Am the author and finisher of your faith.

Shine Your Light

*"14 "You are the light of the world. A city that is set on a hill cannot be hidden.15 Nor do they light a lamp and put it under a basket, but on a lamp stand, and it gives light to all who are in the house.16 Let your light so shine before men, that they may see your good works and glorify your Father in heaven."
Matthew 5:14-16*

Because I Am the light of the world and I dwell in you, I have made you the light of the world. So Shine! Shine bright. Let others see Me in you. Shine your light. Don't hide it.

Delight Yourself in Me

" Delight yourself also in the LORD, And He shall give you the desires of your heart." Psalm 37:4

Sing –Praise – Worship – Proclaim My name to the nations. Delight in My ways. Delight yourself in Me. Draw near to Me and know that I Am your God. Do not look to the left or to the right. But keep your eyes fully focused on Me. You will rise in this hour as you take steps forward in My kingdom. I Am opening doors of effectual service. Get ready – walk forward and know that I Am God. Look and see the things that I Am doing. Look and follow Me as I lead you into all truth. I will guide you by My Spirit. I will change you, transform you and make you a joy to all people as they see Me in you. Give and do not withhold. Give and I will bless and multiply all that you give. I will give you favor and a new anointing. I will give you My Word that will encourage and strengthen you and others in this hour. Preach My Word and do not hold back. Out of the treasures of your heart –your mouth will speak. These should not be hidden treasures, but treasures freely given out of a heart of love.

Guard Your Heart

" Keep your heart with all diligence, For out of it spring the issues of life." Proverbs 4:23

Bring Me your heart – for out of it flows the issues of life. Guard your heart for many things try to enter. What you allow in your heart will eventually flow out of your heart. So fill your heart with My Word, My Ways, My Love, My wisdom. Fill your heart with Me.

I Am The Lord Your Healer

"I am the LORD who heals you." Exodus 15:26

I will make a way for you where there seems to be no way. My hand is not short that it cannot save. I will protect and raise you up in this hour. You will not be touched by the devourer. Instead I will turn all things for your good and My glory. Bring to Me your offerings of praise and lay them at My feet. Know that I Am God and there is no other. I Am the Lord your God and I fail not. I Am the Lord your healer and I fail not. I Am the Lord your strength and nothing will be impossible for Me! I Am your deliverer and there is no other. I Am your strong tower, your shield and your refuge. I Am that I Am and there is no other, I Am.

The Path of Life

" You will show me the path of life; In Your presence is fullness of joy; At Your right hand are pleasures forevermore." Psalm 16:11

Bring to Me your offerings. I will direct your paths. I will show you the path of life. In My presence you will know joy. You will walk with me in the high places. I will walk with you every day. Hear Me in the small things as well as the big things. I will make a way for you where there seems to be no way. Draw near to Me and I will draw near to you. Know that I Am God. Know that I Am your king. Sing, sing, sing and make music with your whole heart. Draw near to Me, draw near to Me, draw near to Me and I will draw near to you. Sing, sing, sing and draw near to Me. Sing, sing, sing and know that I Am God. I Am your God, I Am your strength. Sing, sing, sing.

I Will Never Leave You

"For He Himself has said, "I will never leave you nor forsake you." Hebrews 13:5

Do not fret. I Am always with you. I will take you through the issues of life. I will make a way for you where there seems to be no way. Look to Me and know that I Am God. I will never leave you or forsake you. So rest in Me and walk with the full assurance of My love. Place every issue of life one by one into My able hands. I Am able to do all things and I will do those things that are necessary for My purposes to be fulfilled. Know that I already have a plan for all things. I will keep and fulfill My promises in you. Know that I Am God and there is no other.

Do Not Be Afraid

"The LORD is my light and my salvation; Whom shall I fear? The LORD is the strength of my life; Of whom shall I be afraid?" Psalm 27:1

Are you afraid? Do not fear for I Am with you. I will bring My light to light your darkness. I will deliver you from every situation that you face. Did I not teach you to trust Me in every situation? So why are you fearful now? Have I left My throne? Am I not God? I Am able to deliver you and to keep you in My loving care. Look up. Look up. Take your eyes off the circumstances and fully fix them on Me. I Am your solid rock. I Am your shield and protector. I will take you the distance. You will finish your call and destiny in Me. Nothing will be able to hold you back, kick you down and rob you of My presence and My blessings. I Am your God forever. So do not fear. I Am surely with you.

Trust In The Name of The Lord

"Some trust in chariots, and some in horses; But we will remember the name of the LORD our God." Psalm 20:7

I will bring My release in this hour as I pour out My Spirit on all flesh. Like a river I will overflow My people and they will be saturated in My love. Nothing will be impossible to those who believe. Nothing! So look to Me and rejoice in My presence. Rejoice in My love. Trust in Me and walk according to My Word and My ways. Delight yourself in Me. I will bring to pass My purposes in you. Some trust in chariots and some in horses. But for those who trust in the name of the Lord will be over comers, triumphant and victorious.

Now Is The Day of Salvation

"Behold, now is the accepted time; behold, now is the day of salvation." 2 Corinthians 6:2

Now is the time for salvation. I have opened the floodgates and I have poured out My Spirit upon all flesh. This is the harvest time. This is the time of the ingathering. I have prepared My people in this hour to reach the lost. Open your mouth wide and I will fill it. I will do a work in and through you. Do not hold back and do not hesitate. I Am with you and I will use you for My glory. Do not waver and waste time. Time is valuable and must be used to its fullest potential. Go forth now and touch the hurting and I will pour out My healing salve through you. I love you. Now bring to Me your offering. Bring to Me your life. Bring to Me your gifts and talents. Allow Me to anoint and appoint you to effectual service in My kingdom. Come, do not waste time. Come!

Sacrifice of Praise

"Therefore by Him let us continually offer the sacrifice of praise to God, that is, the fruit of our lips, giving thanks to His name." Hebrews 13:15

Draw near to Me for I desire to speak to you and instruct you in the ways that you should go. Bring your offering, the sacrifice of praise. Release all that I have placed in your heart into My hands. I will keep you in all My ways. I will instruct you in the ways of righteousness. I Am your God and there is no other. I Am your strength and I will fill you with every good thing. Be diligent and pursue those things that will bring glory to My name. Pursue those things that will advance My kingdom. Follow hard after Me. I Am your God and there is no other. I Am your strength and I will lift you up and carry you through the trials, storms and difficulties of life. I Am that I Am and nothing is impossible for Me.

The Love of God In You

"Now hope does not disappoint, because the love of God has been poured out in our hearts by the Holy Spirit who was given to us." Romans 5:5

This is the day of restoration. I Am bringing My people to a fullness of My presence and love. I have declared that the love of God is shed abroad in your hearts by the Holy Spirit who is in you! Now rejoice for the paths of the righteous are ordered by Me. I have set a plain path before you. I have given My promises and I Am faithful to watch over them and fulfill them. I will in the days to come open the windows of heaven and there will be showers of blessing. You have built your faith on sure foundation and nothing can separate you from My love. Nothing! I Am with you always.

I Do Not Lie

"God is not a man, that He should lie" Numbers 23:19

Celebrate! For all I have said – That will I do! I do not lie. I tell you the truth. I Am the Ancient of Days. I stand upon the circle of the earth. I Am the Sovereign Lord! I reign in power and authority. Who will declare My words? Who will make Me known among the nations? Declare My words. Heal the sick. Feed the poor. Restore the backslider. I have commissioned you to be My mouth piece. Open your mouth wide and I will fill it. I will fill it. I will fill it.

Signs Will Follow

"And they went out and preached everywhere, the Lord working with them and confirming the word through the accompanying signs. Amen." Mark 16:20

Listen to Me for I desire to speak to you. I desire to walk with you. I will fill you with good things. I will make you glorious in this season – for I will impart to you the essence of My being. When you touch the world they will experience My touch. I will flow through you and I will transform you. I will always make a way for you. So trust Me in the small things and trust me in the large things. I Am entrusting you with My Word. Do not hold back. Do not waste time. Souls are in the balance and the only means of deliverance is My salvation. Go forth and speak My Word and signs will follow My Word. Lives will be changed for My glory. I will work through you My marvelous works. Many will be drawn to Me. Be obedient and open your mouth wide and I will fill it. Signs, wonders and miracles will follow the preaching of My Word. Preach, Teach and lead the world to Me. I'm waiting.

Make Known My Faithfulness

"I will sing of the mercies of the LORD forever; With my mouth will I make known Your faithfulness to all generations." Psalm 89:1

Now is the time to stand and proclaim My goodness throughout the earth. Now is the time to shine your light, My light to all the people of the earth. Know that I Am God and I Am moving in the earth. I Am taking the ground that the enemy has tried to steal. The ground that the wills of men have foolishly given away. I Am re-taking that which is rightfully mine. I legally bought it back by shedding My pure life blood for the souls of people. Go now gather the harvest. Go now proclaim my goodness throughout the earth. Listen closely as I instruct you in the way that you should go. I will bring to pass My purposes in your life. You will rejoice because of the great harvest that is coming in. You will celebrate with joy for all the good fruit that will remain for eternity. Souls redeemed, renewed and restored. All for My glory. All for My kingdom.

Trust Me With Your Whole Heart

"5 Trust in the LORD with all your heart, And lean not on your own understanding; 6 In all your ways acknowledge Him, And He shall direct your paths." Proverbs 3:5,6

Do not rely on your own understanding. Your perception of the things that you see. Instead trust Me even when you cannot see Me involved in a situation. Know that I Am God and I Am able to do all things perfectly and always in My own timing. Acknowledge who I Am and I will direct your paths. I already have a solution to the problem. Let your heart rest in confidence. Waiting on My timing for all things

Prophesy

*"Prophesy to the breath, prophesy, son of man, and say to the breath, 'Thus says the Lord GOD:"Come from the four winds, O breath, and breathe on these slain, that they may live."
Ezekiel 37:9*

Prophesy to the wind. Proclaim My dominion and authority in the earth. I have made you a diadem in my crown I have lifted you up from the pit. I have clothed you in My robes of righteousness. Draw near to Me and I will draw near to you. I Am coming soon. I Am gathering the precious fruits of the earth. I Am gathering you with My love. Do not be afraid, for the hearts of men will fail them for fear of all that is coming on the earth. But you keep your heart before Me and do not fear. I have you in the palm of My hand. In the cleft of the rock. I have you in My loving care. I will never leave you or forsake you. I Am your God and there is no other.

Your Labor Is Not In Vain

" Therefore, my beloved brethren, be steadfast, immovable, always abounding in the work of the Lord, knowing that your labor is not in vain in the Lord." 1 Corinthians 15:58

Bring Me your praise. Rejoice in My presence. I Am changing things. Did I not declare it? I Am pouring out blessings where there has been adversity. Yes, you will see fruit for your labor. For your labor is not in vain. But for My glory. I will equip you. Keep your eyes and your heart fully focused on Me. I desire faithfulness on the inward parts. For out of your heart flows all the issues of life. I Am with you in mighty power. I Am with you to protect and comfort you. I love you with an everlasting love. I love you. Draw near to me and know that I Am God.

The Crooked Places Made Straight

" I will go before you And make the crooked places straight.."
Isaiah 45:2

Listen carefully to My words. I will instruct you in the way you should go. I will prosper you in My purposes. I will cause the fire of My Spirit to ignite My church. I will in this hour pour out My Spirit in a greater measure. You will see adversity move out of the way. You will walk in victory. I Am bringing a refreshing and you will know that I Am God. Renew your vision, renew your strength. For I have not forgotten you. I have been molding and shaping you. I will give you My heart in this hour. You will know victory where there has been defeat. Lift up your eyes to me. Do not waver. I Am changing all things and bringing about My purposes. Lift your eyes to Me. Look to Me. For in Me is life, life abundant, life complete. I will bring wholeness, healing and My purposes to pass. I will change your life and make the crooked places straight. I will empower you. I will breathe new life in you. I will change you for My glory. Lift up your eyes to Me. Stay completely focused on My ways and I will prosper you. Rejoice for I Am with you in great measure. I love you.

Goodness And Mercy

"Surely goodness and mercy shall follow me All the days of my life.." Psalm 23:6

I have gone before you preparing the way. My grace will keep you in the days ahead. Remember that My goodness and mercy go with you wherever you go. So look to the days ahead with expectancy knowing that I have prepared for you everything that you will need in this hour. Trust Me and rest.

You Are More Than A Conqueror

"Yet in all these things we are more than conquerors through Him who loved us." Romans 8:37

My Word will instruct you in the way you should go. I Am bringing to pass My purposes in your life. I Am empowering you to be victorious and an over comer. I Am filling you with My Spirit. I Am making a way for you in this hour. Rejoice, be glad, shout aloud, for I Am blessing you in this hour. I Am moving in your life. I Am bringing you to the house of victory. You are victorious and more than a conqueror in Me!

Give And It Will Be Given To You

"Give, and it will be given to you: good measure, pressed down, shaken together, and running over will be put into your bosom. For with the same measure that you use, it will be measured back to you." Luke 6:38

Give and it will be given to you. Good measure pressed down and running over. I Am working in you by My Spirit. I Am bringing My presence in a greater way. Wait on Me. Listen, yield and trust Me. I Am your Solid Rock. I Am your strength. I will fill you to overflowing. I will take you from glory to glory. I will create in you a clean heart. I will RESTORE all that the devil has stolen and replace it with more and better than before. I love you My child. I love you. I love you. As you give – it will be given back to you. Give freely. Give lavishly. Give more than you think you can give. Why? Because you can never out give Me. I have promised that with the same measure you give it will be measured back to you. I Am waiting to bless you. What are you waiting for? GIVE!

Hunger and Thirst For Me

" Blessed are those who hunger and thirst for righteousness, For they shall be filled." Matthew 5:6

I Am your God. I Am at work in you. I have heard the cry of your heart. As you hunger for more of Me and My ways I will reveal Myself to you in a greater measure. I will change you from glory to glory. Sing a new song. Sing a song of love, for I will your heart with the music of heaven. I will renew your mind and your strength. Trust in Me and know that I Am God and I hold all things in my hands. Bring to Me the sacrifice of praise and I will draw nearer to you in this hour. I will break every yoke off your life. I will remove those things that hinder you. I will reveal Myself to you in a greater measure in this hour. I Am changing you from glory to glory by My Spirit. Acknowledge Me in all your ways and I will direct your steps.

The Desires of The Flesh

" I say then: Walk in the Spirit, and you shall not fulfill the lust of the flesh." Galatians 5:16

Bring your offerings to Me and present them with a pure heart. Present them with a clean heart. I desire to work in you that I would be glorified in you. So walk in My Spirit and you will not fulfill the desires of your flesh. Walk with Me and listen to My voice. I desire that you would seek Me with your whole heart. Seek Me and know that I Am God. Success lies with those who are obedient to My Word and My ways. So follow Me and I will do great and mighty works in you. I will supply your every need. I Am your God and your strength forever.

Care For Others

" Let each of you look out not only for his own interests, but also for the interests of others" Philippians 2:4.

I have chosen you that you would bring forth My purposes in the earth. There are many who only look out for their own needs. There are many who do not take the time to care for the needs of others nor My kingdom. I have formed you and called you that you would proclaim My goodness throughout the earth. I Am your God. I have called you to Myself. Look to Me and trust Me that I will lead you by My Spirit. I will draw you closer to Me in this hour. I will instruct you in all My ways. Follow hard after Me. I will make a way for you and I will supply all your need. Call forth the blessings and dispatch My angels to gather them from the four corners of the earth. I love you and care about every detail of your life. So sow your seeds and I will bring a great harvest to you. Sow your seeds.

The Glories of Heaven

" Immediately I was in the Spirit; and behold, a throne set in heaven, and one sat on the throne" Revelation 4:2

Come into My presence and experience the glories of heaven. I will manifest myself to you in this hour. One second in My presence will change you for a lifetime. Leave the cares of this life behind and draw near to Me. In Me you will find joy unspeakable and full of glory. I will cause the stench of this world to fall off of you. You will find your total fulfillment in Me. Delight in Me. I Am the treasure of your heart forever. The one who truly loves you.

Many False Prophets

" Beloved, do not believe every spirit, but test the spirits, whether they are of God; because many false prophets have gone out into the world." 1 John 4:1

Listen to the words I have to say. Listen to My voice. There are many false prophets who have risen in this world. Their message appears to be credible because they speak truths. But the truth is mixed with deception. Do not be taken in by such voices. For I Am your foundation of truth. Walk in love and let love motivate the things that you do. Know that I Am God and there is no other. I Am your strength and you need not look to another. Walk with Me. Obey My voice and I will unfold My blessings in abundance. Put all things in order in your life and get ready. For there are many I desire to touch through you.

I Am Doing A New Thing

" 18 "Do not remember the former things, Nor consider the things of old. 19 Behold, I will do a new thing, Now it shall spring forth; Shall you not know it? I will even make a road in the wilderness And rivers in the desert." Isaiah 43:18,19

You are My child. I chose you. I made a way for you. Today marks a hallmark in your life. I Am bringing you into a deeper walk with Me than ever before. Do not consider the things of old. Do not remember the former things. I will do a new thing in your life. I will make a way for you where there seems to be no way. I will draw you near to My side. Listen to My voice and I will lead you every day. I will make you a blessing and will give you a great harvest. This is harvest time. Get ready for I will use you to touch many lives.

I Will Fight Your Battles

" For the LORD your God is He who goes with you, to fight for you against your enemies, to save you." Deuteronomy 20:4

I will fight your battles for you. Trust Me and rely on My Spirit. Is anything too hard for Me? Embrace My love and let My love be a shield around about you. Let My love saturate and permeate your soul. For I truly love you. Do not ever doubt My love for you.

Soar Upon My Promises

"But those who wait on the LORD Shall renew their strength; They shall mount up with wings like eagles" Isaiah 40:31

My Word is a lamp unto your feet and a light unto your path. Listen closely to My instructions for I will lead you by My Spirit into all truth. I will give you the ability to rise on wings as of the wings of an eagle. Soar upon My promises and rise up above those things that would try to hinder you. I Am your God and there is no other. I Am your strength. Put your trust in Me. Walk with Me. I Am with you in Spirit and in Truth. Give and it will be given to you, good measure – pressed down, shaken together and running over shall men give into your bosom! Give and I will give back to you in a greater measure. Trust Me and I will supply all your need. I Am your God and I will lead you by My Spirit. I Am your strength forever. Look to Me. Trust in Me and know I Am able to do all things in my perfect ways and timing for all matters. I love you! Rest in My love. Trust in My love and be filled with My love

The Rock of Our Salvation

"Oh come, let us sing to the LORD! Let us shout joyfully to the Rock of our salvation." Psalm 95:1

Bring your offerings of praise and enter into My presence. Let your spirit arise and bring under submission your flesh. Trust in Me and know that I Am God. Nothing shall be impossible for me. For I Am your rock and your salvation. I Am your hope and song. Today is a good day. Enjoy this day and don't be robbed of My blessings. I desire to bless you and for you to walk with Me. My ways are so far above your ways. So be prepared to move with Me when I say move, when I say go, when I say stop. Listen and you will be blessed.

Obedience Brings You Closer

"Behold, to obey is better than sacrifice,..." 1 Samuel 15:22

Listen closely and do not be afraid. For the things I tell you to do, you will be blessed when you are obedient. I will bring you closer to Me in this hour that you would know and understand My heartbeat. There is a rhythm and a pattern that will put you in sync with Me. Draw near I say, draw near. Remove all the distractions and draw near. My Word will cleanse you and purify you and give you clear direction. Draw near I say, draw near. To obey is better than sacrifice. I will give you the ability to obey Me in all things. Yield to My Spirit and let Me change you and you will find the strength and wisdom you need to follow Me with your whole heart.

Forget The Past

" Brethren, I do not count myself to have apprehended; but one thing I do, forgetting those things which are behind and reaching forward to those things which are ahead,14 I press toward the goal for the prize of the upward call of God in Christ Jesus." Philippians 3:13,14

A new beginning I give to you. Do not let the past dictate what you do today. Learn and glean knowledge from the past, but do not let it hold you back from fulfilling your call that I have for you today. Today is a good day. A day to worship, to follow, to obey, to accomplish all I have called you to accomplish. Look to Me and do not let your feelings hold you down or hold you back. Do not let your enemy intimidate you and make you feel you are always falling short. Have confidence towards Me and know I Am with you. I will order your steps even this day. So be prepared and know I Am going to bless you. You are my delight. I love you with an everlasting love. A love that cannot and will not be taken from you. I Am your God and there is no other. I speak and all things are held together by Me. I Am the victor! Your triumphant king. I will slay the wicked and preserve My people. Go and pierce the darkness. I have made you an over comer. So go forward in My kingdom purposes. I love you.

"20 For if our heart condemns us, God is greater than our heart, and knows all things.21 Beloved, if our heart does not condemn us, we have confidence toward God."
1 John 3:20-22

Dig Again The Wells

"And Isaac dug again the wells of water which they had dug in the days of Abraham his father, for the Philistines had stopped them up after the death of Abraham. He called them by the names which his father had called them."
Genesis 26:18

I Am your God and I Am your strength. Look to Me for all things. This is an hour that I Am pouring out My Spirit upon all flesh. I Am bringing a refreshing where there has been a dry parched barren land. I will restore life and I will unstop the wells that have been stopped up. My child, re-dig the wells. Remove those things that hinder the flow of My presence in your life. Let Me burn up the dross and cleanse your temple. For I Am a God of renewal. A God of love and a God of victory. My will and My purpose for your life is to raise you up as a light in this hour to shine bright in the darkness. To shine bright in this world. That those who are faltering and failing may be drawn to the light. I Am rising in you in a greater measure. Get ready for I Am opening new doors to you and those doors will be doors of blessing. That you may rise up in this hour to accomplish that which I have purposed even before the foundations of the earth were laid. Begin to look for those open doors. I will open your eyes that you may walk forward in My kingdom purposes.

"'These things says He who is holy, He who is true, "He who has the key of David, He who opens and no one shuts, and shuts and no one opens": 8 "I know your works. See, I have set before you an open door, and no one can shut it; for you have a little strength, have kept My word, and have not denied My name." Revelation 3:7,8

Walk According To The Spirit

"there is therefore now no condemnation to those who are in Christ Jesus, who do not walk according to the flesh, but according to the Spirit." Romans 8:1

I will renew your strength. I desire that you walk according to My Spirit and not according to your flesh. I will fill you to overflowing and I will transform your mind. My Word will arise in strength and My power will break every chain that tries to bind you. So look up-fix your eyes on Me. Do not look at your circumstances. I Am greater than all these. But instead –look to Me. I will intervene in all these situations and I will bring victory where it has looked impossible. I Am coming to you in this hour in My mighty power and strength. I Am bringing you to the place of victory where you will soar like an eagle. Walk with Me and I will speak to you. I will give you clear direction and make a way for you where there seems to be no way. I Am the way maker. My ability to bring about My purposes cannot be hindered. I Am God and there is no other. I Am your God. I will strengthen you. Renew you. Restore you and you will fulfill your call and destiny. You will cross the finish line in mY strength. In My time. In My power. So rejoice and go forward in My purposes for you.

"Now to Him who is able to keep you from stumbling,
And to present you faultless Before the presence of His glory with exceeding joy, 25 To God our Savior, Who alone is wise, Be glory and majesty, Dominion and power, Both now and forever. Amen." Jude 24,25

Prepare For Famine

"Behold, the days are coming," says the Lord GOD, "That I will send a famine on the land, Not a famine of bread, Nor a thirst for water, But of hearing the words of the LORD."
Amos 8:11

My child – attend to My words. Listen and obey. For a time will come when there will be a famine of the Word of God in the land. People will desire words that pacify their fleshly desires. But you must hide My word in your heart. You must meditate on it day and night. Put your trust and your faith in Me and not the wisdom of man. For My ways are far above your ways and My thoughts above your thoughts. Put your trust in Me and do not waver. Sound doctrine is necessary for a complete and balanced life and ministry. So listen carefully and do not be misled by trends and tactics of the world. When I told Peter to throw the net on the other side of the boat it did not make sense to him, an experience fisherman. But he said. "Never the less, at Your Word." When he was obedient he received the blessing when he least expected it. I will do the same for you. I Am opening doors in ministry, in business and in your walk with Me. You will be prosperous in all these things. Just be obedient. Not delayed obedience. But when I tell you to do something, do it and do not procrastinate. Do it and you will reap a great harvest for My kingdom. A harvest of plenty, a harvest of blessing. I Am the God of the harvest. The time is now. The harvest is ready. Go forward and do not hesitate. I will provide for you. You will lack nothing. I will make a way for you. Get yourself ready. Prepare the ground. Prepare the way of the Lord. Prepare your heart

The Breath of My Spirit

"And when He had said this, He breathed on them, and said to them, "Receive the Holy Spirit" John 20:22.

Vibrant – I will breathe new life into you. I breathed on My disciples and they received My Spirit and power. I will breathe new life into you. Release those things that hinder and hold you back. Release those things that hold you down and look to Me. For I Am the author and finisher of your faith. I Am your deliverer. Bring every issue of life to Me and lay them at My feet. I will consume them with My fire. Through the fire the things that I desire to remain will remain. Those things that I desire to remove from your life will be consumed. I Am an all consuming fire.

The Treasure of Your Heart

"For where your treasure is, there your heart will be also." Matthew 6:21

The treasure of your heart will always be Me. I will not allow the enemy to deceive you and to take you out of My hand. I have placed you securely in the palm of My hand. Learn to delight in Me and all My ways. I will fill you every day with My goodness. Whatever you do, do it with all your heart to Me. I will bless the work of your hands and give you favor. Do not fret over those who do not respond to My call. If they reject Me , they will reject you. Pray for them and entrust them in to My care. I Am God and there is no other.

The Just Live By Faith

"Now the just shall live by faith; But if anyone draws back, My soul has no pleasure in him." Hebrews 10:38

The just shall live by faith. Give unto Me the glory due My name. Worship Me in spirit and in truth. I Am giving you the opportunity to serve Me in My fields of harvest. Take up the sickle and begin to harvest the lost and bring them into the safety of My grace, mercy and lovingkindness. They need the true breath of life. I will take care of you. I will lead you by My Spirit says God. My grace is sufficient for you and My strength is made perfect in your weakness. Rely on Me. Trust and do not be shaken. For I Am the Lord your God and I fail not. I will gather My people from the four corners of the earth and there will be rejoicing like there never has been before. I Am moving sovereignly and who will stop Me? Who can stop Me? I made the worlds. I formed them. And I have the power to destroy them. I Am working on your behalf and you will know liberty and strength. The power of God at work in you. Do not be discouraged. Get up and do what is right in My sight. Receive My promises – They are yes and amen!

Whoever Touches You

"Keep me as the apple of Your eye; Hide me under the shadow of Your wings." Psalm 17:8

Whoever touches you, touches the apple of My eye. I will protect you. I will defend you. I will comfort you. I will heal you. I will hold you and hide you under the shadow of my wings. You can rest in Me, for I Am your shield and protector. I will not allow anyone or anything to harm you.

Rejoice!

"I will be glad and rejoice in You; I will sing praise to Your name, O Most High." Psalm 9:2

This is a day of celebration. You will and you can celebrate My abundant provision. Foe I Am Yaweh Yireh – The Lord your provider. I have prepared a place of provision for you. You will excel in My power and My strength. Delight yourself in Me. I Am the Alpha and Omega. The beginning and the end. I Am the God that heals you. I Am He who turned the water into wine and I will turn your impossible situation into abundance. So rejoice, for the steps of the righteous are ordered of the Lord.

I Am Love

"And we have known and believed the love that God has for us. God is love, and he who abides in love abides in God, and God in him." 1 John 4:16

Now – today is the day of salvation. Many souls are weighing in the balance. Who will go for Me? Who will tell them that I Am the way, the truth and the life? Bring them to Me – for I Am gentle, loving and kind and I will embrace them. I will heal them. I will comfort them. I Am a just God and I Am the king and ruler of the universe. But I Am love. I created love. It is the very essence of who I Am. Love is the highest and best and I will lavish you and My people with My love. Look to Me for all good things. I will not withhold it from you. But I freely give of Myself to you. Be filled with all the fullness of God. Be filled with My love.

I Will Fight For You

" The LORD will fight for you, and you shall hold your peace." Exodus 14:14

My word is a lamp to your feet and a light to your path. Do not fear what the enemy would try to do to you. I Am your rock and strength and no harm will come near your dwelling. I Am the one who fights your battles. I will defeat your enemies. Just put your trust in Me. I Am your God and there is no other. I Am your strength. Look to Me and know I will take you the distance. You will walk in victory. You will walk in my love. Sing a song of victory and do not be discouraged. I Am your God and I will fight your battles. Rest in Me. Trust in Me and submit to Me. I will fill you with My peace and I will refresh and re-new your strength. I love you. Receive My love this day and walk in it.

Yield and Be Obedient

" If you are willing and obedient, You shall eat the good of the land." Isaiah 1:19

I will bring you into My plan and purpose for your life. You will discover that I have prepared things even before you knew My plan. I will unfold My manifold wisdom in your heart and life and you will walk in high places with Me. Do not resist My Spirit , but yield and be obedient and I will walk you close to Me. I will open doors and you will be blessed. Trust Me and know that I Am God. I love you. I will make a way for you. Be ready and obedient and you will always walk in My abundance. Be ready and do not falter, but trust Me completely in all things.

A Land of Milk and Honey

"He has brought us to this place and has given us this land, a land flowing with milk and honey" Deuteronomy 26:9

I will bring you into a land that flows with milk and honey. I will make a way for you. I Am your God and there is no other. Release those things that hinder you and embrace those things that I have given you. Sing, shout, praise and rejoice – for I Am your deliverer and I will deliver you from every snare and the sin that does so easily beset you. I will infuse you with My strength. I will fill you with My Spirit and you will see dumbfounding miracles as I move in this hour and season of the earth. I will set My people free and they will rejoice in Me.

Work While it is Day

"I must work the works of Him who sent Me while it is day; the night is coming when no one can work." John 9:4

Work while it is day. For the time will come when no one will be able to work and bring in the harvest anymore. Souls are weighing in the balance. Many are ready but no one will go to them. Quick – mobilize and strategize and make a plan to reach the lost. I will equip you with every tool you need. I Am the Lord of the harvest. Preach My Word. Teach My Word and walk with me. I will bring to pass My kingdom purposes in you. Look up, for I Am coming soon, Look up and not at your circumstances. Seek Me with all your heart. Seek Me and you will find Me. I Am not standing aloof or afar from you. But I Am near you, longing for you, desiring your obedience to Me. So go! Don't look back. GO!

I Will Bless You

"Surely blessing I will bless you, and multiplying I will multiply you." Hebrews 6:14

I will bless you beyond all that could dream or ask Me for. I will redeem you and deliver you from the snares of the enemy. I Am your God and there is no other. Bring to Me your offerings of praise. Lay your burdens at My altar of love. Know I Am working all things together for your good and My glory. I love you and desire to bring you into the fullness of your calling. I Am your God and your strength. My Word is a lamp unto your feet and a light unto your path. I Am your deliverer and I will make a way for you every day. For My plan for you is progressive and purposeful. My plan is unfolding for you even in this hour. I will move heaven and earth on your behalf. So look to Me and trust Me for the highest and best for your life. I Am your God and there is no other.

I Will Not Withhold My Love

"No good thing will He withhold from those who walk uprightly." Psalm 84:11

I Am bringing you into My presence to share in a more intimate walk. I have heard the cry of your heart and I have seen your desire to draw near to Me. I will not withhold My love or My presence from you. But I will embrace you in this hour. I will cover you and protect you. I Am your rock and your strength. Look to Me. Trust Me and know that I Am God. Open your ears and your heart towards Me and receive instruction. I will lead you into all truth. I Am your God and I fail not. I Am wrapping you in My arms of love. I Love you.

I Work Among a Perverse Generation

"That you may become blameless and harmless, children of God without fault in the midst of a crooked and perverse generation, among whom you shine as lights in the world." Philippians 2:15

My child I Am at work in the earth. My heart is for you and I can and will work wonders in the midst of a perverse generation. Do not get caught up in the spirit of this world. But hide yourself in Me. Saturate your heart, life and ministry with the Word of God. I Am your God and heaven and earth will pass away but My Word will abide forever. Proclaim My goodness throughout the land. I Am your God and your strength forever and ever. I Am your everything and source of life. Trust Me and walk in obedience with me.

Bring Me a Sacrifice of Praise

"Therefore by Him let us continually offer the sacrifice of praise to God, that is, the fruit of our lips, giving thanks to His name." Hebrews 13:15

Bring to Me your sacrifice of praise. Bring to Me your offerings. I will bless and multiply back to you everything you have need of. I Am your source of your total supply. I will bring you into My blessings and you will overflow with abundance. I will show you a more excellent way. Look to Me and rest in My love. I Am your God and your strength. I raise up and put down. Know that I will raise you up in this hour to speak of My ways. I Am making a way for you in this hour. Rejoice and rest in My love and you in Me. I Am your rock and your salvation.

I Am Your Deliverer

"The LORD is my rock and my fortress and my deliverer; My God, my strength, in whom I will trust." Psalm 18:2

Now is the time. Now is the time – to rise up and conquer all those things that have held you back from accomplishing My purposes. I Am your God and strength. I will make a way for you in this hour. Walk with Me and know that I Am God. I Am your deliverer. Rejoice and be glad for victory is here. I Am the God of victory and victory is here. Rejoice, rejoice, rejoice. I will make a way for you where there seems to be no way. Rejoice, victory is here. Rejoice.

New Things I Declare

"Behold, the former things have come to pass, And new things I declare; Before they spring forth I tell you of them."

Today is the day that I have created. I Am moving through the earth. I Am bringing about My kingdom purposes. This is an hour that many will try to rise up and stop the Gospel. But I Am greater than all these attacks. I will have My way in the earth. Who can stop Me? I Am God and there is no other. I Am King and I have dominion over all things. Worship Me and lift up My name to the nations. I will change all things for MY glory. I will fill your heart with good things. Listen to My voice and put your trust in Me. I will order your steps. I will lead you by My Spirit. Rejoice and be glad for the former things have come to pass and new things I declare. I Am your God and there is no other. I Am your King.

I Make All Things New

"Behold, I make all things new" Revelation 21:5

Bring to Me all the issues of life. I have the ability to change all things. Trust Me and know that I will work all things together for your good. Do not be afraid for I Am with you. I make all things new. My mercies are renewed every morning and great is My faithfulness. I Am bringing you to that place in Me where you will enter into My rest. That you will trust Me for all things knowing that I Am almighty. Look to me for every decision and every step you make. I will make all things new. I will take you to the finish line. I will work on your behalf to transform all things. Nothing is too hard for Me. I can transform any life and situation no matter how much deterioration has taken place . Nothing is impossible for Me- Nothing.

Cease From Your Dead Works

"How much more shall the blood of Christ, who through the eternal Spirit offered Himself without spot to God, cleanse your conscience from dead works to serve the living God?" Hebrews 9:14

My Word will light your pathway. I Am bringing you to a place in Me where you will cease from your dead works and be fruitful and productive in My kingdom. I Am your strength and deliverer. Multitudes of souls are crying out for deliverance but trying to find peace through the temporary things of this world. Shine your light and bring hope to the nations. Prepare your heart and life to follow Me in obedience. You will eat of the fruit of your labors in Me.

I Am The Way

"Jesus said to him, "I am the way, the truth, and the life. No one comes to the Father except through Me." John 14:6

Now is the acceptable time. Today is the day of salvation. You must see and feel the burden of My heart for the lost. Know that My hand is extended to reach the lost. Let My love guide you. Let the desires of My heart be your desires. For time is short and time will not wait for others. Now is the acceptable time. Use every day to the fullest. Use every day for My glory. Many souls are at a cross roads without answers. They are seeking solutions for their problems. But they do not know that I Am the truth, I Am the life, I Am the way. So that they may be free. I Am pouring out My Spirit on all mankind. This is a great hour and this is the day of salvation. It is harvest time. Get out into the fields and work for Me. I will open the doors and I will make provision for you. Look to Me for all things. Look to Me.

I Reveal My Glory

"For the earth will be filled with the knowledge of the glory of the LORD, as the waters cover the sea."Habakkuk 2:14

These are the days of My mighty outpouring. These are the days of renewal. I will pour out My Spirit on all mankind. I Am opening the floodgates and releasing signs, wonders and miracles. I will influence and change nations. I will arise in this hour. My glory will be revealed and My glory will cover the earth as the waters cover the seas. I Am filling the earth with My love and My manifest presence. It is time to arise and do not hold back any longer. Arise run into My embrace. Arise. I have released My blessings in your life and ministry.

Now is the Day of Salvation

"Behold, now is the accepted time; behold, now is the day of salvation." 2 Corinthians 6:2

Now is the day of salvation. The fields are ripe for harvest. Lift your eyes to see the great harvest. I have prepared it. Just as the fruits of the earth come to fruition, so does the souls of men. My spirit has watered the seed of the Word and now it is harvest time. Do not let the precious fruit drop to the ground and rot. But work from morning until night to gather the ripe fruits. I will lead you and use you to gather in a great harvest. I Am preparing you and making a way for you. Do not be distracted by the cares of this life. But focus on Me, My Word and My kingdom. I will enlighten you and show you great and mighty things that you do not know. Wait for Me. Wait on Me. Wait I say and I will reveal all things in My way and My timing. Wait I say on the Lord.

My Word Abides Forever

"Heaven and earth will pass away, but My words will by no means pass away." Luke 21:33

Make melody in your heart to Me. Sing aloud with songs of adoration. I Am bringing you to a place in Me where you will no longer struggle with the issues of life. But you will rest in Me and find comfort in My promises. Heaven and earth will pass away but My Word will abide forever. I keep My Word and the decisions that others make contrary to My will cannot stop Me from fulfilling My Word. I will bring you to that place in Me where you will find rest. I will take you through every difficulty of life and will shine My light on your pathway. Know that I Am God and your portion forever.

Justified Through My Blood

"24 Being justified freely by His grace through the redemption that is in Christ Jesus, 25 whom God set forth as a propitiation by His blood." Romans 3:24,25

I justify you through My blood. I will cleanse you and remove every hindering force in your life. I Am bringing you to that place in Me that you will walk in holiness and purity of heart and mind. My Word will instruct you. Let the words of your mouth and the meditations of your heart be acceptable to me. Whatever things are pure, honest of a good report think on these things. Dwell upon My promises and know I will fulfill My Word concerning you and your household. Put your focus and eyes on Me. I Am the author and finisher of your faith.

I Will Fill You With Good Things

"Many are the afflictions of the righteous, But the LORD delivers him out of them all." Psalm 34:19

Draw near to Me with a heart of worship. Bring your offering of praise and lay it at My feet. For I delight in the aroma of one who pours their heart and love upon Me. I desire the sweetness of your life. I will embrace you in this hour. I will fill you with good things. Many are the afflictions of the righteous but I will deliver you out of them all. For I love you and I see and know all things. I know the motives of the heart. Keep your heart pure before Me and walk in love. My love will transform and renew your mind daily and will draw you closer to Me in intimacy.

Rest and Quietly Trust

*"It is good that one should hope and wait quietly
For the salvation of the LORD." Lamentations 3:26*

I Am bringing you to a place in Me that you can rest and quietly trust. A place where you will cease from any striving or anxiousness. I hold all things in My hands and I have a season for all things. Get ready for this season that I am moving you into. Preparation and obedience will bring great fruit for MY glory. My love for you is everlasting. Draw near to Me in this hour and rest in My love. I Am the God of Abraham, Isaac and Jacob. I Am your God. Look to Me for all things. All things will work together for your good and My glory.

Don't Wait For Perfect Conditions

"If you wait for perfect conditions, you will never get anything done." Ecclesiastes 11:4 TLB

The harvest is great but the laborers are few. Who will go for Me? I say lift up your eyes and look and you will see that many are lost and need those who will lead them to Me. Will you go for Me? Will you trust Me for your every need? Do not waste time and do not wait for perfect conditions. For if you wait for perfect conditions you will not get anything done. Instead put your trust in Me and know that I Am God. I will work all things together for your good and My glory. I will supply all your need. I Am just waiting for you.

I Am Your Protector

"My lovingkindness and my fortress, My high tower and my deliverer, My shield and the one in whom I take refuge.."
Psalm 144:2

Look to Me for strength, for guidance and instruction. You will find in Me all you need to walk in the high places. Soaring above your circumstances and dwelling in My presence. I will be your high tower. Your protector from the fowler. Your shield in times of trouble. Though the storms rage – My peace will dominate every fiber of your being. Though time seems to never end, I will come quickly. You will stand in awe of Me. You will rejoice before Me because I will move swiftly and surely and all that I have promised and all I have ordained will come to pass. HALLELUJAH!

Time Is Short

"But this I say, brethren, the time is short..."
1 Corinthians 7:29

My child, I have a work for you to do. It is a good work. I will give you the ability to carry out the tasks I desire to do through you. I will give you the strength and you will know that I keep My promises. I will not go back on My Word. But time is short and there is much work to be accomplished. My Word will be fulfilled. The earth will know the glory of God. The earth will see My power manifested. Open your eyes. Sharpen your vision. See the plan and purpose I have for you. Revival, restoration – I will touch the hearts of many. You need to be available for My use and you will know the greatness of your God. You will know that it is I who leads you and guides you and makes your footsteps sure.

I Will Restore

"Restore us, O God; Cause Your face to shine, And we shall be saved!" Psalm 80:3

My child, the sun rises and sets – but my love will never set. It will shine continually. I will be your strength and I will be your God. I gave the heavens and the earth. I spoke them into existence. Is anything too hard for Me? Am I not greater than any circumstance that would stand in your way? I will come quickly and restore all that the enemy has taken from you and more. For I delight in you and I know My thoughts and My plans I have for you. I have not forgotten, nor will I. For My love for you is enduring. It will never fail. I love you with all that I have and all that I Am. Delight yourself in Me. I will give you the desires of your heart.

You Are My Chosen

"I have made a covenant with My chosen, I have sworn to My servant David." Psalm 89:3

Bring Me your praise. Bring Me a heart of worship. Open your heart to me and know I will bring My abiding presence. I desire to dwell in your midst. You are My chosen. You are My beloved. I have betrothed you to myself. Draw near to Me and listen. Do not be distracted. Do not look upon another for I Am your life. I Am your hope. I Am your love. I dwell in the midst of My people. Remember that I called you. I will equip you. I will fight your battles. For they are My battles also. I will work in a greater measure than you know how to ask Me for. I love you!

Abundance

"And God is able to make all grace abound toward you, that you, always having all sufficiency in all things, may have an abundance for every good work." 2 Corinthians 9:8

Now is the time. Listen carefully to My guidance in all things. I am bringing you into a season of abundance. But you must listen for I have specific plans for every provision. The temptation will be there to go in directions I have not purposed and ordained. You must seek to keep your heart in obedience to Me and My voice as I speak and guide you into all truth. Look to Me and walk in the fullness of My blessing. Many souls are weighing in the balance and many are headed down the path of destruction. Who will go for Me? Who will speak for Me? I have been forming you. I have been making a way for you even in contrary circumstances. So do not be afraid and do not falter in this hour. Bur rise in My strength and wisdom. Walk in complete obedience and you will experience My abundant blessings as I propel you forward in My plan for your life. Rejoice for this is a great hour and season. A season of abundance and a season of the harvest.

I Do Not Condemn You

"20 For if our heart condemns us, God is greater than our heart, and knows all things. 21 Beloved, if our heart does not condemn us, we have confidence toward God." 1 John 3:20,21

I do not condemn you – so why do you condemn yourself? I know what you have done and I know what you have been through. But I have forgiven you. So forgive yourself. Have confidence in your relationship with Me. I am for you and not against you. Your past is gone. I Am with you always.

The Divine Nature

"By which have been given to us exceedingly great and precious promises, that through these you may be partakers of the divine nature, having escaped the corruption that is in the world through lust". 2 Peter 1:4

New opportunities are on the horizon and some are here now. Prepare your heart and mind and rise to the occasion to pursue these opportunities. Do not turn back. I Am your rock and your strength forever. Know that I Am bringing you to a place in Me where you will believe for the impossible and break through the impenetrable situations. I Am changing you. The way you think. The way you talk. The way you walk. I Am developing in you the divine nature that others will see Me in you. You are My ambassador. So represent Me the true representation of who I Am.

Rejoice In Me Always

" Rejoice in the Lord always. Again I will say, rejoice! Philippians 4:4

Lift up your voice in song to Me. Receive the joy of heaven into your environment. I will fill every part of your being with the glories of heaven. The realm of My Spirit in you will increase and the cares of this world will decrease. You will know Me in a deeper and fuller dimension. I Am accelerating the move of My Spirit around the world. My people will walk in the supernatural realm and will experience My intervention on many levels. Keep singing. Keep rejoicing and keep walking in faith. For that which seemed impossible will be possible for you because of My great power at work in you. I Love you and I Am with you always.

About The Author

Dr. Rick Kurnow

Rick was raised in a Jewish home. He went to Hebrew school and had his Bar Mitzvah. When he was 13 his family moved to Hawaii. At age 17 a Japanese friend pointed Him to his Messiah Yeshua (Jesus). Ricks life was radically changed when he invited Yeshua into his life. That was in 1974. He immediately knew he had a call on his life and entered Bethany Bible College in Santa Cruz, California. He received a Bachelor of Science degree as a ministerial major. Rick met his wife Dottie at Bible College and they were married in 1978. Together they have ministered in churches and traveled for over 33 years. Rick has been mightily used of God to impact many lives. The gifts of the Holy Spirit flow richly through his ministry. In 2005 Rick received a Doctor of Divinity from The School of Bible Theology Seminary and University in San Jacinto, California, Dr. Kurnow currently resides in Corona California where he Co-pastors with his wife Dottie, Gates of Praise Worship Center in Ontario, California. Also Rick and Dottie frequently speak and minister throughout the USA and Mexico through Kurnow Ministries International. You can find out more about their ministry at *www.Kurnow.org*

Dr's Rick & Dottie Kurnow

Rick is also a recording artist with the release of 3 music CD's recorded with his wife Dottie. His most recent CD is "Here Comes a Miracle." He is also the designer of the New Covenant Messianic Tallit Prayer Shawl. Thousands of these prayer shawls have touched lives all over the world. Dr. Kurnow's DVD teachings "The Biblical use of the Shofar", "The Biblical Use of The Tallit" and "Yeshua Revealed in the Passover" has been distributed all over the world and has been a blessing to many. Also Rick is the author of the books "Supernatural is Natural" Volume 1 – The Blessings of Hearing the Voice of God - Volume 2- Signs, Wonders and Miracles and "Learning To Love God's Way. These books are also available in Spanish.

Rick & Dottie are the founders of Shofars From Afar, LLC a company that supports the economy of Israel by offering Jewish, Messianic and Christian products. These unique gifts can be found at *www.ShofarsFromAfar.com*

Made in the USA
Middletown, DE
22 February 2019